# SPEED BUMPS
## ON THE ROAD TO INTIMACY
## WITH GOD

*How To Transform Your*
***PRAYER MONOLOGUE** into a*
***PRAYER DIALOGUE.***

*Slow Down For Speed Bumps!*

*Mike Landry*

## BY MIKE LANDRY

# TABLE OF CONTENTS

# DEDICATION

**Dedication to my children**

First, I want to thank my children who were more committed to my success as a writer than I was. They believed in me and took that belief to the next level.

As a Christmas present, my children and their spouses chose to give me an amazing and totally unexpected gift. Jason and Amanda, Beth and Steve, and Michelle and Nathan chose one of my sermon series from a few years back and transcribed 6 messages that would eventually evolve into this book. They did some editing and had it published for my private viewing as a Christmas gift a couple years ago.

They had been encouraging me to write a book for some time and decided this would be just the right way to jump start that process. I have never before seen such an expression of love, commitment, and generosity. This unselfish act was amazing and demonstrated an exhausting commitment and investment in my success as a writer. I've been slowly editing it for the past couple years in my free time and am now ready to give them back a copy of the finished book.

Thanks kids for believing in me and loving me in a way I'll never forget or get over. I love you too.

**Dedication to my wife**

My wife Cindy has persistently encouraged me to write for years. The gift from my children was just the opportunity she needed to give me that extra nudge. Thank you Hon for allowing me to use our vacations over the past two years as times to edit and write this book. Your patience and loving nudges have helped me enormously to fulfill one of my dreams.

## Dedication to a few others

I pastor a church full of people who encourage me. Many have asked me to put into writing what I teach them week after week. To these people I want to thank. As I wrote and rewrote this book, I had you in mind.

I also want to thank Stephanie Hayes and Christy McGuire for their help with some of the editing. Their positive input kept me on track and added much needed clarity as I faced editing "speed bumps" in the writing process.

## Dedication to My Lord Jesus

This book is a reflection of my own spiritual growth journey. The longer I have followed Jesus Christ, the more I have grown to love Him. He has faithfully placed speed bumps in my life and they have forced me to slow down and pay attention to Him. I thank Him for not letting me settle for less in my relationship with Him. I also thank Him for helping me to articulate so many of the lessons He has taught me about intimacy with God. I pray he will be able to use this book to help others maneuver over their speed bumps and grow closer to Him.

## CHAPTER 1

# TRANSFORMING YOUR PRAYER MONOLOGUE INTO A PRAYER DIALOGUE

Communication is the essence of any relationship. Ongoing conversations peel away the mysterious layers of an individual's personality and open the door to true friendship and intimacy. Without conversations, relationships dry up and become lifeless.

Suppose you were married and never said to your spouse, "I love you." This void in communication would surely raise doubts of your love to your spouse. It would strain your relationship rather than strengthen it. Suppose you had a friend and only talked about the weather. This kind of rapport would never lead to meaningful and intimate companionship.

*Without conversations, relationships dry up and become lifeless.*

There must be an exchange of words, ideas, hopes, dreams, and feelings to enhance a relationship. These principles seem obvious when it comes to your relationships with other people, but what about your relationship with God? Is it possible for you to interact with God as intimately as you do others?

God has revealed Himself as relational. This is particularly clear as we look at how Jesus related to others. God created you with everything needed to enjoy and nourish a relationship with Him. He has also preemptively dealt with the one thing that prevents you from experiencing a personal and intimate relationship with Him. We will discuss this often throughout the book. It may not seem like it, but the most common obstacle to this kind of relationship with God boils down to your choice not to participate in the relationship. It is tragically that simple.

God earnestly desires to have an everlasting and eternal relationship with you! However, you may be failing to cultivate honest, open, and meaningful communication with Him simply because you do not know how. Or perhaps your good intentions fall short of the close connection you desire with God. The busyness and rapid speed of your life may often cause you to drive past an intimate relationship with God. I believe God purposefully places speed bumps in our lives to get our attention and slow us down long enough to establish or repair a broken relationship with Him.

The Bible has many examples of people who sped through life and ran into God's strategically placed speed bumps. They were forced to slow down and examine their relationship with God. When heeded, it enabled them to experience the kind of relationship with God they were created for. I think you will see that there is much we can learn from taking a closer look at their lives. Every one of these snapshots will focus on their ability, or inability, to clearly communicate with God.

*God purposefully places speed bumps in our lives to get our attention and slow us down long enough to establish or repair a broken relationship with Him.*

The Bible specifically calls communication with God "prayer." Unfortunately, when most people hear the word "prayer," they immediately think of a religious monologue aimed at God. Prayer is most often thought of as a means to deliver requests to God. It is perceived as being one-sided – a time for you to speak and a time for God to listen. But communication, by definition, must be two-sided.

Prayer is intended to be a dialogue with God—an exchange between you and God—that changes you and draws you nearer to Him. It is the biblical prescription for intimacy with God. Prayer literally changes the way you see God and cultivates a kindred spirit between you and God. Prayer is a time to become transparently honest and vulnerable with God. It is also a time when you can expect God to reveal Himself and open up to you. When you speak to God, you can expect Him to respond; in turn, He also will expect a response from you.

Throughout the Bible, God initiated many intimate relationships with people. He walked as a companion to Adam in the Garden of Eden during the cool of the evenings. God listened as Abraham boldly expressed his concerns about the destructive plans for the city of Sodom. God spoke directly to Moses through a burning bush, revealing His name. Jesus invested three-and-a-half years developing relationships with His disciples as He daily shared His thoughts, insights, and plans with them. You'll want to be sure not only to take note of these episodes of communication between God and man, but also to learn from their examples. Intimacy and friendship with God are within reach!

This book is dedicated to helping you connect and develop intimacy with God by examining some of the interesting relationships that God had with some very familiar Biblical characters. You will observe how their relationships with God began and developed. You will examine their lives and the ongoing conversations that led to an intimate relationship with God. These conversations, or *Prayer Dialogues,* will encourage and empower you to grow deeper in your own relationship with God.

*Intimacy and friendship with God are within reach!*

At times, these *Prayer Dialogues* will reveal shining examples of what a faithful friend of God looks like. At other times,

9

they will give a glimpse of some of the everyday blunders that Christians often make as they attempt to get closer to God. However, in my opinion, one of the greatest lessons you will learn is that you don't have to be perfect to have a vibrant and growing relationship with God. As you look at how flawed and imperfect these biblical characters are, you will be encouraged when you see that God desired to connect with them. And God desires to connect with you, too! The good news is that He desires a relationship with you more than you do. He will do whatever is needed to enable you to come into this relationship without forcing you to do so.

In the following pages, the lives of seven people will be examined: Abraham and Sarah, Joshua, Jacob, Nehemiah, Ananias, and Gideon. Each person relates so differently to God. Their stories will illustrate the nature of a prayer dialogue and teach what it takes to develop an intimate relationship with Him. I encourage you to read and familiarize yourself with their entire stories in the Bible as you read the brief snapshots of their lives that are highlighted in this book.

> *You don't have to be perfect to have a vibrant and growing relationship with God.*

Be forewarned that this is not a book intended to make you feel comfortable or satisfied in your walk with Christ. You will discover what enhances and what deteriorates your relationship with God. You can expect to become uncomfortable as you realize that the lack of intimacy with God is the result of *your* unwillingness to slow down at the speed bumps and engage in a dialogue with God.

But do not despair or become discouraged! Knowing the truth about your current relationship with God, no matter how painful that may prove to be, allows you to begin the restoration process in that relationship. You cannot get any closer to Him as long as you tolerate things in your life that blocks intimacy with God.

Spiritual growth and intimacy with God is His plan for your life. You can expect Him to do whatever it takes to get your attention. It will be an amazing journey. I can tell you from experience that, if you are willing, you are about to embark on the most incredible ride of your life. You'll want to be sure to fasten your seat belt. I believe the truths you find illustrated in this book will help.

*God is waiting to talk with you. Go ahead and start the conversation.*

My desire is that you will use the faith God has given you (*no matter how small it may be*), buckle up and go through the door that God has opened just for you.

Finally, as you read this book, take time to pray. Let your prayer evolve into a dialogue with God. Ask God questions like these:

- *"What have You been trying to say to me?"*
- *"What do You want me to do in light of what I have just read?"*
- *"What is hindering me from getting closer to You?"*
- *"How can I grow in my conversations with You?"*
- *"Is there a speed bump ahead that I need to slow down for?"*

In fact, take this moment to pray. Ask God to give you new eyes to see and apply the lessons you are about to learn from these *Prayer Dialogues*. Your relationship with God will become much more intimate as you apply the principles you are learning.

God is waiting to talk with you. Go ahead and start the conversation.

## QUESTIONS FOR PERSONAL EVALUATION AND DISCUSSION:

1. What does communication look like within your earthly relationships? Do you feel like communicating with God is an unattainable goal?
2. What are some areas of your life that are hindering an open communicating relationship with God?
3. Share an example of one way, you feel, God has communicated with you? Be specific.

## PRAYER:

*Heavenly Father, I know I am prone to doing all the talking in my prayers. Help me to turn my Prayer Monologue into a Prayer Dialogue and start listening to You. Please speak to me as I read the following chapters about men and women who knew how to effectively communicate with you.*

*Chapter 2*

# TAKING GOD SERIOUSLY: ABRAHAM AND SARAH

As a pastor I regularly counsel people who have just placed their faith in Jesus Christ and received Him as their personal Savior and Lord. They always have many questions concerning this new relationship with God. Some of them come from Christian homes with parents who are wonderful spiritual role models; however, they are still unsure about how to grow in their relationship with God. Others come from non-Christian homes and have no clue about where to even begin on their new path. They have an insatiable hunger for spiritual matters and would like to have a vibrant, personal, and growing relationship with God, but they don't how to proceed. That's how I began my journey.

Today, I am a follower of Jesus Christ, but that was not always the case. Years ago when I enrolled as a student at Georgia Tech, I was a professing atheist. It was difficult for me to take God seriously. In fact, I wasn't even sure there was a God. My first prayer started with, "God, *if* You are up there ..."

I wanted to know God **IF** He could be known. But I wasn't sure how it worked. I knew only one person who seemed to have what I was looking for. This friend challenged me to read the Bible for the answers to my questions. Eventually, I took him up on his suggestion. I secretly read the four Gospels in the New Testament and came to the conclusion that the Bible was not the book of rules I had thought it was. For the first time, I read and understood that God desired a relationship with me and that He had paved the way for me to have forgiveness, grace, and eternal life through the death and resurrection of Jesus Christ. It was at that moment when I realized I needed to respond to God's initiative.

Since that time I have met many others who have placed their faith in Jesus Christ and are growing in that relationship. These people have engaged in an authentic and intimate relationship with God rather than merely being committed to a list of religious practices. They take God seriously. That was what I was looking for as a college student. I wanted to know God; I wanted to be able to take Him seriously. I was not interested in becoming religious. Do you want to know God and take Him seriously? I think you'll find some helpful lessons to be learned from the *Prayer Dialogue* of Abraham and Sarah.

### *The Speed Bump: Taking God Seriously*

In the twelfth chapter of Genesis, God abruptly told Abraham, a seventy-five-year-old man, to pack up all of his possessions and move his family from the place he had called home. Where was Abraham to go? His destination was yet to be disclosed. God assured him that more information about his destination would come later. God also promised to bless Abraham and bless all nations through his descendants; even though at the time Abraham and his sixty-five-year-old wife, Sarah, were childless.

*These people have engaged in an authentic and intimate relationship with God rather than merely being committed to a list of religious practices.*

So Abraham obeyed God; he gathered his family, his servants, and all his possessions and left for an unknown destination. Shortly thereafter, God spoke to Abraham again, reminding him that the nations will be blessed through his children. God revealed that Abraham and Sarah would have a child through whom all the nations would be blessed.

Can you imagine what must have been going on in Abraham's mind during this time? It is amazing that he did as God had instructed. After one short encounter with God, Abraham agreed to obey the vague instructions requiring he leave the comfort of his home and take his family to a yet-to-be revealed location. In addition, he had been told that his wife, who was beyond childbearing years and had been barren all of her life, would give birth to a child. Not only would Sarah bear a child, but this child and his descendants will prove to be a blessing to all nations. Abraham did not need every detail of God's plan; the few details were enough for Abraham to take God seriously and obey His command. Abraham and Sarah traveled for the next ten years, following God's lead.

Thoughts of uncertainty and doubt prevailed, as they began to question what God really meant years earlier. Sarah had yet to bear the child whom God had promised, so they began to consider other options. Perhaps God meant for the child to come another way than through Sarah. After all, she was seventy-five-years old!

Sarah didn't believe she could bear children anymore and suggested that Abraham take her handmaiden, Hagar, and have a child through her. Abraham initially had reservations about her plan but eventually agreed. A child was born and was named Ishmael. This compromise of God's intended plan resulted in many problems for Abraham and Sarah. (In fact, it has caused problems for the descendents of Abraham to this day.) Abraham and Sarah were merely trying to "help" God accomplish His plan. They genuinely thought this might have been what God intended. In effect, they ceased taking God seriously.

For four years, both Abraham and Sarah continued to think that this child, Ishmael, was the one God had intended. Then God spoke to Abraham and reminded him of the promise to bless all nations through "his seed."

Abraham thought, "Of course, God, You mean Ishmael."

15

To which God retorted, "Ishmael is not the son to whom I am referring. I never intended for you to have a child with another woman than Sarah. My plan is for you and Sarah to conceive a child."

Abraham was surprised by God's response. He reminded God that he was now ninety-nine years old and that Sarah was eighty-nine—having a child at their ages was impossible! How quickly Abraham concluded that he knew better than God. However, God continued to be gracious and patient with the couple.

God replied to Abraham's skepticism and doubt with a reminder that He would do as He promised in the exact way He intended. God told Abraham that Sarah would be pregnant before he would hear from God again. A few months passed: Sarah was pregnant, and God indeed showed up again.

### God Is Speaking In The Speed Bump

The previous summary of the conversations with God and Abraham took place over twenty-five years. During those encounters, Abraham sometimes trusted and obeyed God completely, and sometimes he did not. There were times when he perfectly understood God's instructions, and there were times when he did not. However, throughout this time span, Abraham was learning that God was God. The closer Abraham got to God and the more he learned about God only clarified who God was. This is the most important lesson of a prayer dialogue. Conversations with God require slowing down long enough to take God seriously. Thus, the importance of God's strategically placed speed bumps.

*Conversations with God require slowing down long enough to take God seriously.*

So, how are you to take God seriously? The next few pages will highlight how Abraham did this and how you can follow his example.

16

## *How To Make The Most of This Speed Bump*
**1. Take God seriously by regularly returning to designated holy ground sites.**

Quite often, when God met with someone in the Old Testament, the place was thereafter referred to as a holy place or "holy ground." Sometimes an individual, such as Moses in Exodus 3 or Joshua in Joshua 5, were told at the moment of their encounter with God to take off their shoes because the ground where they were standing was "holy." At other times, sites became designated as "holy" after the encounter. Altars were constructed upon the holy ground after such an encounter with God had occurred. When they would pass the altar in the future, it would remind them of their past dialogues with God and often prompt another conversation. At other times, an individual would plan a trip to the holy place in hopes that God would speak again.

Abraham returned to such an altar to reflect upon the previous twenty-five years, from the time God commanded him to leave his home until the time Sarah bore a son. Returning to this altar prompted Abraham to remember all that God had accomplished and said the last time he was there.

Abraham had first built this altar at Hebron decades before when he had parted with his nephew, Lot. Before they had parted ways, Abraham and Lot lived in unity, both prospering greatly. However, as their flocks multiplied exponentially, they began to argue about where each of their herds would graze. Abraham suggested they separate rather than destroy the family unity. He told Lot to choose the land he preferred and take his family and flocks there; Abraham would then take his flocks elsewhere.

Immediately following Lot's departure, Abraham constructed an altar in order to offer thanks to God. Genesis 13:18 says, *"Then Abram moved his tent and came and dwelt by the oaks of Mamre, which are in Hebron, and there he built an altar to the LORD."* Twenty-five years later, Abraham came back to the altar he had built at the oaks of Mamre at Hebron, where he very likely reminisced the former times there with his nephew, the incident of separation, and the promises that God had made to him. He returned to holy ground hoping to have another prayer dialogue with God. He was not disappointed.

> *"Now the LORD appeared to him by the oaks of Mamre, while he was sitting at the tent door in the heat of the day. ² When he lifted up his eyes and looked, behold, three men were standing opposite him; and when he saw them, he ran from the tent door to meet them and bowed himself to the earth, ³ and said, "My Lord, if now I have found favor in Your sight, please do not pass Your servant by."* (Genesis 18:1-3 NASB).

Abraham hoped that God would show up again. And He did! The three men who arrived are later identified in Scripture as two angels and God. (Genesis 18:8, 22, 19:1) When they arrived Abraham ran to meet them, imploring them to spend some time with him in his tent. He knew there was something special about this moment. He made the most of it; he chose to take God seriously.

One of the many ways you can take God seriously is by marking places or occasions when you have previously met with God. When God speaks with you, first make a mental note of it. Then record the mental note on something like a journal, a picture, a plaque with a memory verse, and so forth. You will later find the markers to be helpful in remembering past conversations with God and, like a speed bump, they will slow you down long enough to continue your dialogue with Him.

I've made such markers in my own life. Sometimes, I write in my journal so that I can later remember what God taught me on a particular occasion. Other times, I revisit specific places where I have built mental altars that have become holy places in my life. When I travel there, whether physically or mentally, I am reminded of what God did in my life.

For example, one holy place for me is in Hinesville, Georgia. When I was in high school, my father was stationed at Fort Stewart, Georgia. Shortly after I graduated, he left for Vietnam. My mom and I moved to Hinesville so I could attend a college in Atlanta. The next year, I became a Christian during my summer break from college. On that "holy ground" in Hinesville, I began my *Prayer Dialogue* with God, and a spiritual foundation for intimacy with God was established. I am always encouraged when I remember the changes God brought about in me at that place and time. In fact, every time I drive north on Interstate I-95 toward Savannah and pass the sign that says "Hinesville/Ft. Stewart 12 miles" I am reminded of what God did in my life and I find myself refocusing and taking God seriously again.

My personal spiritual marker reminds me of past conversations with God and creates a desire for more dialogue. It keeps my conversation with God fresh and encourages me to know Him more. It gives me perspective–that God has brought me a long way from my atheistic past. It reminds me that He is not finished with me yet!

God wants you to designate spiritual markers. God wants you to remember the special places where He has spoken to you, changed you, taught you, restored you, or healed you. It can be anywhere—the beach, the park, a church building, or even a tree, such as in Abraham's experience. Every time you go to or are reminded of that place, it should prompt you to take God seriously

*He has changed you and plans to continually work in you and on you to shape you for His purpose and glory.*

and continue the conversation with Him. The location is simply a beacon to help you stay focused on what you really want: an ongoing and genuine conversation with God. Be careful not to elevate the physical location so that it actually becomes more important than God. Taking God seriously means taking *God* seriously.

Committing to memory all that God has done for you in the past and having it so indelibly engraved in your life reminds you that God is not yet finished. He desires to fulfill His purpose in you in your current situation and for the rest of eternity. He has changed you and plans to continually work in you and on you to shape you for His purpose and glory.

Sometimes returning to your spiritual marker or altar can be painful as you are reminded of God's discipline or correction. Perhaps going back to the holy ground can simply be an exercise in patience and waiting on God. In Abraham's case, he was waiting at the entrance of his tent in the heat of the day. Surely, it was unpleasant waiting, but he was determined to spend time on holy ground seeking God's presence and continuing the dialogue.

### 2. Take God seriously by predisposing yourself to serve God— anytime and anywhere.

When you are at your spiritual marker, whether physically or mentally, and God shows up, immediately respond to Him. Let Him know you have been fervently waiting for this moment. Demonstrate your eagerness with a willingness to serve Him anytime and anywhere.

Abraham couldn't have illustrated this more clearly.

> "So Abraham hurried into the tent to Sarah, and said, "Quickly, prepare three measures of fine flour, knead it and make bread cakes."
> [7] Abraham also ran to the herd, and took a tender and choice calf and gave it to the servant, and he hurried to prepare it. [8] He took curds and milk and the calf which he had prepared, and placed it

20

*before them; and he was standing by them under the tree as they ate." Genesis 18:6-8*

Note that as soon as Abraham saw the three visitors, he eagerly became their servant. He did not wait for them to ask for anything; he grasped the opportunity to serve them.

Taking God seriously means you understand and fully accept the role of a servant. Never forget the difference between you and God. He is always God; you are always His servant. God has uniquely created you with the capacity to know Him and to love Him—and He desires for you to know Him and love Him more. He

> *Taking God seriously means you understand and fully accept the role of a servant.*

has also invited you to be a vital part of His plans. But these privileges should never distort the distinction between who you are and who God is. He is God—you are not.

When Jesus came to earth, His agenda was to serve, not to be served (Matthew 20:28). The intimacy between Jesus and the Father was demonstrated by Jesus' unwavering commitment to do only what He "saw His Father do" (John 5:19). His unconditional love was demonstrated in the practical ways He served others. He gave of Himself so that all might live. That is who He is.

Yet, Jesus' servant role is often misunderstood. It is tempting to minimize the nature and role of Jesus as God when you see Him living with a servant's heart. However, just because He came to serve humanity doesn't make Him any less God. In fact, His role as a servant is a reflection of His nature. God is love; therefore, Jesus is love. Love reveals itself through service. You can always expect God's agenda to include acts of service.

Consequently, to walk with God is to join Him as He serves others. Your intimacy with God is enhanced when you serve others. If you are not serving God, then there is a troubling disconnect between you and Him. His agenda is one of service. Take God seriously by living like a servant.

I saw this principle lived out through the initiative of our church chef. He and his crew prepared 6,000 cookies to donate to the nursing staff at a large local hospital on "Nurse Appreciation Day." The church enthusiastically embraced Chef Ric's plans and offered to help. People volunteered to bake, package, and deliver the cookies; others showed up at the hospital to greet and thank the first shift of nurses. Another large contingent of volunteers arrived later to deliver cookies and express gratitude to the next shift of nurses. Everyone involved—from the church members who were serving, to the nurses who were being served—was energized!

There is something invigorating about expressing and demonstrating gratitude by serving others. When you find yourself serving others, you are emulating the very heart and agenda of God. Whenever you serve others, you are taking God and your relationship with Him very seriously.

Matthew 20:26-28 says,

> *"On the contrary, whoever wants to become great among you must be your servant, and whoever wants to be first among you must be your slave; just as the Son of Man did not come to be served, but to serve, and to give His life-a ransom for many."*

Taking God seriously is revealed by your willingness to serve.

### 3. Take God seriously by refusing to compromise even when His plan sounds impossible.

Have you ever tried to change God's plan if it doesn't fit into your own plans? Abraham and Sarah were guilty of this. Read what happened when they were reminded of God's plans by the three visitors in Genesis 18:9-15:

> "Then they said to him, "Where is Sarah your wife?" And he said, "There, in the tent." [10] He said, "I will surely return to you at this time next year; and behold, Sarah your wife will have a son." And Sarah was listening at the tent door, which was behind him. [11] Now Abraham and Sarah were old, advanced in age; Sarah was past childbearing. [12] Sarah laughed to herself, saying, "After I have become old, shall I have pleasure, my lord being old also?" [13] And the LORD said to Abraham, "Why did Sarah laugh, saying, 'Shall I indeed bear a child, when I am so old?' [14] "Is anything too difficult for the LORD? At the appointed time I will return to you, at this time next year, and Sarah will have a son." [15] Sarah denied it however, saying, "I did not laugh"; for she was afraid. And He said, "No, but you did laugh."

Sarah laughed at the absurdity of God's plan. Why? Because there was no way she or Abraham could accomplish it by themselves. They couldn't do it even if they wanted to! So they chose to take matters upon themselves, defer to "Plan B," and find someone else to bear Abraham's child.

Compromise seems so much easier than obeying God, especially when His plan requires the miraculous and it is not clear as to how or when God will accomplish that plan. Most people want to be able to explain and control everything. Planning and acting prudently should be the norm; however, when God says He is going to do something, He is not limited by your physical abilities, your plans, or your capability to understand. God is not expecting you to understand *how* or *when* He will accomplish His plans. God simply wants you to trust Him. Trusting Him means you are taking Him seriously.

After ten years of waiting for the fulfillment of God's promise, Sarah began to wonder, "*It's been a long time. Maybe God meant that we were supposed to do something about this ourselves. Since I haven't been able to get pregnant, perhaps I need to find a woman who can bear Abraham's child and fulfill God's plan."*

That's compromise. God was very clear and specific about what He was going to do. Abraham and Sarah were frustrated because they could not understand how it was possible and tried to accomplish His supernatural promise in their own power. God insists that you take Him seriously by refusing to compromise when His perfect plan seems impossible to your human limitations.

> *When God says He is going to do something, He is not limited by your physical abilities, your plans, or your capability to understand.*

Jesus dealt with this issue on several occasions. Once, He talked about how difficult it was for a rich man to enter into the kingdom of God and compared it to a camel going through the eye of the needle. The disciples responded, *"Jesus, if it really is that difficult then nobody will ever get in. It's impossible!"* Jesus replied, *"What is impossible with men is possible with God."* (Luke 18:27)

The real problem is that you start speeding through life so fast that you forget who God is. When you take God seriously, you are choosing to believe that God is God; and that He, by nature, is able to accomplish the impossible. When you understand and believe that God is God, you won't have difficulty believing He can do the impossible.

Have you ever felt like Abraham and Sarah? Have you ever tried to rationalize God's plan by substituting your own because you couldn't figure out how He would do it? Have you forgotten who God is? Is it possible to get close to God after you have messed up, doubted Him, and refused to believe Him?

Yes. God understands and still loves you. In fact, despite all that Abraham did, God still calls Abraham a "friend of God". (James 2:23)

How can you avoid compromising God's plan? What can you do to stop from replacing God's plan with your own? How can you trust God when what He promises seems so impossible? There are three lessons to learn from what Abraham did that are very helpful when faced with just such questions.

- **When you are faced with the impossible, remember God's nature.**

    Genesis 18:13-14 says, *"And the LORD said to Abraham, "Why did Sarah laugh, saying, 'Shall I indeed bear a child, when I am so old?' [14] "Is anything too difficult for the LORD? At the appointed time I will return to you, at this time next year, and Sarah will have a son.'"*

    Imagine the absurdity of the conversation between Abraham and God. Abraham told God what was and was not possible. Did he not realize he was talking to the Creator of the universe, who is able simply to speak anything into existence? God is never limited (unless it is a self-imposed limitation like the incarnation of Christ—see Philippians 2:6-8). God, by nature, can do anything.

    > *When you doubt God's abilities, it is likely you have forgotten that He is God.*

    When you doubt God's abilities, it is likely you have forgotten that He is God. When you find yourself doubting God, take a moment and remind yourself of His nature. Stop equating Him with yourself and your abilities. Stop defining Him within the confines of your limited understanding. God is God, and you will never be able to adequately describe Him.

- **When you are faced with the impossible, count on God to always keep His promises.**

It is important to know what God is promising. God had promised Abraham a child. Later, He added the details. Abraham and Sarah were later informed when the child was to be born, so they could make final preparations. The upcoming birth of Abraham and Sarah's coming child was not a figment of their imagination or wishful thinking. They had heard directly from God and were taking Him seriously by clinging to His promise.

The Scriptures are full of God's promises. But, of course, you will never know what God's promises are unless you take time to read the Bible. Taking God seriously will require a disciplined lifestyle of Scripture intake. God will begin to speak to you through His Word. Then get ready! When God makes you a promise, you can count on it; God will never break His promise. Continually offer prayers of gratitude for what God intends to do. Your faith will be exercised and strengthened when you trust God to keep His promises.

- **When you are faced with the impossible, refuse to become skeptical.**

Skepticism can destroy faith. That is why God dealt with Sarah in the firm way that He did. He asked her why she laughed, and she quickly tried to deny it. God didn't just let her off the hook. He said, *"No, you did laugh."*

Why did God confront Sarah? Because Sarah didn't just have doubts, she had assumed the role of a skeptic. Sarah wasn't merely laughing; she was scoffing at

> *Skepticism will ultimately cause you to become cynical if you don't pause to take God seriously.*

the very idea of having a baby. It was not only that she didn't understand how God's plan could happen. She didn't believe that it would happen.

26

Skepticism will ultimately cause you to become cynical if you don't pause to take God seriously. Skepticism becomes dangerous when you start acting upon it. It is perfectly fine to dialogue with God and ask questions, but do not allow your doubts to transform you into a resistant, skeptical, and negative critic.

God confronted Sarah's skepticism before it could lead to an attitude and lifestyle of resistance and doubt. Once God speaks to you, do not stain His promise with a tint of skepticism. God's desire is that you accept His promise and proceed to live in anticipation of that promise.

## 4. Take God seriously by faithfully responding when He reveals the rest of His plan.

One of the most surprising parts of Abraham and Sarah's story is that after God dealt with them about the child issue, He immediately proceeded to include them in other items on His agenda. That is so like God! He wants you to be a vital part of His plan and is ready to include you just as soon as you are ready to trust Him.

*Not only does God want you to know what He's doing in your own life, He wants you to know what He's doing all around you!*

Abraham and Sarah had to be ready to change gears. God took them deeper in their faith. Because they were willing to accept the miraculous nature of His plan concerning their child, God was ready to unveil more of His plans with them.

This truth is found in Genesis 18:16-19:

*"Then the men rose up from there, and looked down toward Sodom; and Abraham was walking with them to send them off. [17] The LORD said, "Shall I hide from Abraham what I am about to*

*do, [18] since Abraham will surely become a great and mighty nation, and in him all the nations of the earth will be blessed? [19] "For I have chosen him, so that he may command his children and his household after him to keep the way of the LORD by doing righteousness and justice, so that the LORD may bring upon Abraham what He has spoken about him."*

This is amazing! God wants you to see the big picture. Not only does God want you to know what He's doing in your own life, He wants you to know what He's doing all around you! In fact, He wants to include you in the implementation of those plans.

Abraham was an old man and knew he was very limited in what he was able to do. But to hear these words from God must have been an encouragement to him. God was saying, *"I want you to know that by taking Me seriously, you're going to grow much closer to Me. I also want you to know what I'm planning."* Abraham was

*God is not limited by your gifts or abilities; only your willingness to allow Him to work in and through your life.*

to be the father of a great and powerful nation. God wanted him to know what that meant and what was to be involved.

To take God seriously in this way, you must believe that God designed you to be a vital part of His total plan. You must know that you were not created by mistake; you are not an accident. God made you just the way you are because you are exactly what He needs to accomplish His plan. That's what God says in Genesis 18:19

*"For I have chosen him so that he will command his children and his house after him to keep the*

28

*way of the Lord by doing what is right and just.*
*This is how the Lord will fulfill to Abraham what*
*He promised him."*

God says, "*I have chosen you.*" God has handpicked you to be a part of His plan, even though you may not feel like you can do it. Your competence is not dependent upon your feelings. God chose you! Stop making excuses that you are unfit to do what God is asking. The appropriate and faithful response to God will sound something like this, "I don't get it, but I'm willing." God understands if you don't see how His plan is possible. However, your job is to respond faithfully to Him. Begin by displaying gratitude to God for including you in His plans. Then be willing to go forward with Him with enthusiasm and patience.

This is in contrast to telling God how He can use you. He has the right to use you in any way He desires! Do not evaluate God's assignment based upon your abilities or giftedness. If you don't see yourself as gifted in a certain area, you may conclude that the assignment must not be for you. God is not limited by your gifts or abilities; only your willingness to allow Him to work in and through your life.

Have you considered that God may want to use you in an area that is outside of your giftedness so that you could never take credit for accomplishing it? God is looking for your availability, not your ability.

You must take God seriously by faithfully responding when He reveals His plans to you. Jump in with both feet and say, "Okay, God, I'm willing!"

**5. Take God seriously by asking questions without questioning God.**

As you read further in Genesis 18, it appears that Abraham bargained and negotiated with God. But he was not questioning

God; he was simply asking God questions. There is a difference. Read Genesis 18:20-33 (NASB):

> "And the LORD said, "The outcry of Sodom and Gomorrah is indeed great, and their sin is exceedingly grave. [21] "I will go down now, and see if they have done entirely according to its outcry, which has come to Me; and if not, I will know."
> [22] Then the men turned away from there and went toward Sodom, while Abraham was still standing before the LORD. [23] Abraham came near and said, "Will You indeed sweep away the righteous with the wicked? [24] "Suppose there are fifty righteous within the city; will You indeed sweep it away and not spare the place for the sake of the fifty righteous who are in it? [25] "Far be it from You to do such a thing, to slay the righteous with the wicked, so that the righteous and the wicked are treated alike. Far be it from You! Shall not the Judge of all the earth deal justly?" [26] So the LORD said, "If I find in Sodom fifty righteous within the city, then I will spare the whole place on their account."
> [27] And Abraham replied, "Now behold, I have ventured to speak to the Lord, although I am but dust and ashes. [28] "Suppose the fifty righteous are lacking five, will You destroy the whole city because of five?" And He said, "I will not destroy it if I find forty-five there." [29] He spoke to Him yet again and said, "Suppose forty are found there?" And He said, "I will not do it on account of the forty."
> [30] Then he said, "Oh may the Lord not be angry, and I shall speak; suppose thirty are found there?" And He said, "I will not do it if I find thirty there."

*[31] And he said, "Now behold, I have ventured to speak to the Lord; suppose twenty are found there?" And He said, "I will not destroy it on account of the twenty."*
*[32] Then he said, "Oh may the Lord not be angry, and I shall speak only this once; suppose ten are found there?" And He said, "I will not destroy it on account of the ten."*
*[33] As soon as He had finished speaking to Abraham the LORD departed, and Abraham returned to his place."*

Abraham wasn't questioning God; he was asking God questions. He was trying to make sense of God's plan. He knew that God was both just and merciful. He knew God wouldn't let sin go unpunished; yet, he also remembered how God had redemptively dealt with his own personal sins. Abraham must have questioned, "*How is God going to judge the unrighteous without causing the righteous to suffer unjustly?*"

Abraham was asking questions for clarification. He wasn't saying, "*How dare you, God! How can You even consider doing something like that? Why don't we make a deal here instead? Won't You reconsider?*"

Abraham finally understood when God said He would not bring judgment if He found just ten righteous people in the city. God's answer meant that He had not changed. Abraham didn't need to know everything, but he did need to know that God had not changed. Abraham could take God seriously.

Abraham's nephew Lot and his family lived in Sodom. The angels warned Lot and his family to leave before the city was judged. In fact, the angels had to drag Lot, his wife, and two daughters out of the city because of their reluctance to leave. By doing so, God once again revealed His mercy without compromising His demand for justice.

The two sons-in-law refused to leave and died along with the rest of the city. All the people who were righteous escaped the city while the unrighteous were judged and destroyed. Once again, God remains consistent and faithful to do what He says He will do.

Abraham wanted to take God seriously, but he needed help making sense of this plan. He didn't doubt God's assessment of the situation or disagree with the prescribed judgment. Abraham only wanted to understand God. His desire was intimacy and friendship with God.

God wants you to know who He is and what He is really like. It is so easy to assume the role of a spiritual accountant and start measuring who God is based on the amount of money you have, the number of possessions you have, or the times He has protected you from certain calamities. It is tempting to focus on those things and gauge your intimacy with God by it.

God will never change. His nature is not determined by human circumstances. However, God has various ways of dealing with circumstances. He wants you to take Him seriously; He allows you to ask questions but not to question Him.

I experienced this firsthand. As an atheist, I questioned God, because He didn't make any sense to me. I asked so many questions and had so many doubts: *How could there be so much suffering in the world if there was a God? There must not be a God. If, in fact there is a God, He is a terrible, cruel, and vindictive God.*

While in college, I borrowed a Bible and started reading. It showed me what God was like. I had never seen or heard or read this description of God before. I found myself asking questions instead of questioning God. I started asking God to explain a little bit at a time to me. Finally, it dawned on me that there *may actually* be a God. If so, and if He was like the One I was reading about, then I wanted to know Him. I prayed: *God, if there is a way to know you, I really would like to. I'm willing to come to You on Your terms.*

Even after my prayer, I still was not completely convinced. I continued to have doubts. So I added a little "P.S." to the end of my prayer: *"God, if You're not there, let's just forget this conversation took place."*

I was still full of doubt and confusion, but when I took the first step toward God, it activated my faith. It allowed me to get answers to my questions. These answers led to more questions, which, in turn, led to even more answers. All the while, I was becoming a person who had lots of questions for God instead of ones that questioned Him.

### How will you respond?

When you take God seriously, you can ask Him all the questions you want. He will give you just enough answers to enable you to trust Him and take the next step of faith. Are you ready to take God seriously? A relationship with Him has to start somewhere. The beginning point is up to you. I encourage you to start now.

You have to make the choice, like I did, to take Him seriously and give Him your life. Once you do this, you will learn and see how to take God more seriously in every area of your life.

## QUESTIONS FOR PERSONAL EVALUATION AND DISCUSSION:

1. Take some time and reflect on your journey of faith. Have you fully surrendered to a personal relationship with Jesus Christ? Share your story with a partner about how God has worked in your life and been 'communicating' with you up to this point.
2. Are you *currently* living a life of total trust and belief that "God will do what He says He will do?" Describe the factors that you believe helped Abraham to trust God completely.
3. If the beginning of your salvation and relationship with God begins with a total trust in the finished and

sacrificial work of Jesus Christ on the cross, why are you still prone to doubt God's future involvement and plan in our lives?

**PRAYER:**

*Heavenly Father, I thank You for speaking to me about what it means to take You seriously and demonstrating that through the lives of an elderly couple named Abraham and Sarah. They faced the impossible, but You accomplished the miraculous because they took You seriously. God, help me to take that step of faith and daily to make the decisions required to take You seriously.*

# ABRAHAM AND SARAH

## SPEED BUMPS

- Instructions to leave homeland and go to a yet to be revealed destination
- Delay between promise of a child to the delivery of a child
- Conversation about destruction of Sodom

---

## WHAT IS NECESSARY TO CHANGE YOUR PRAYER MONOLOGUE INTO A PRAYER DIALOGUE?

Take God Seriously

*Chapter 3*

# GOING SOLO WITH GOD: JOSHUA

As a teenager, I looked forward to the first time I would be able to drive a car by myself. With a mere learner's license I was required to be escorted by one of my parents every time I drove. I was nervous the first time I got behind the wheel, but after a few minutes of driving, I knew I was ready to go solo.

After a while, driving with my parents got old. They made me drive so slow, they wouldn't let me listen to the radio, and they wouldn't allow me to have any friends in the car. Boring!

Finally the day came when I got my permanent license and could now drive without one of my parents. They told me that I could drive on my own sometime soon. I was on my best behavior because I didn't want to do anything that would jeopardize my big opportunity.

One day my dad came into my bedroom and threw me the keys to the car. He asked, "How would you like to go to the store and pick something up for me?" I said, "Are you kidding? I'll be glad to get you anything. You know me, Dad, I'm always glad to help."

And then off I went with Dad's perfunctory salutation in the background: "Be careful and don't do anything stupid." I was so excited that I ran to the car. My dad was looking through the window, so I told myself to "be cautious and not blow this opportunity." I buckled my seatbelt, turned on the ignition, adjusted the mirrors, and then slowly backed out of the driveway. Putting the car in drive, I accelerated and was ... driving!

Then it hit me: I'm alone! There's nobody here in the car to correct me, warn me, or slap me alongside the head when I did something dumb. What if I forget something? What if that car coming toward me comes in my lane? What if I run out of gas? Questions, doubts, more questions, fear, and a number of other concerns went through my head. Going solo wasn't as simple as I had thought it would be.

A relationship with God often proves to be a similar experience. Once you engage in a personal relationship with God, your journey usually involves many other people who have already made a similar commitment to God. You may have your parents, Christian friends, pastor, or perhaps a Bible study teacher available to answer your questions, walk alongside you, and cheer you on. The beginning of your spiritual journey is often a team effort.

But then there is a moment in time when you face the speed bump designed for you alone. The dynamic of your relationship with God is about to change for the better. But it will require that you go solo. As you spiritually mature, you may find that you must venture out from the well-packaged form of "Christianity" that seems so popular to everybody. Everyone seems to be headed in the same direction.

> *The "Christian Growth To-Do list" too often becomes a substitute for cultivating your personal relationship with Jesus Christ.*

It's easy to follow when so many others are doing it. The Christian life is easily mistaken for a list of rules and guidelines to live by. The "Christian Growth To-Do list" too often becomes a substitute for cultivating your personal relationship with Jesus Christ. Speed bumps are used by God to get you to slow down and continue the dialogue that cultivates intimacy with

God. Your intimacy with God will not be the result of a spiritual group hug. Eventually you must learn to stand before God and see Him, and Him only, as the One you must please. It's not enough just to be connected with others who know God; you've got to learn to go solo with God.

The reality of your spiritual immaturity and inability to go solo with God is exposed whenever you experience a season of change. Changes in your circumstances, friendships, church, health, finances, etc. will often open you eyes to the shallowness of your own personal faith. You will soon

> *Your intimacy with God will not be the result of a spiritual group hug.*

discover whether your relationship with God was authentic or simply the residue from others who are growing in the faith.

Joshua was faced with a similar situation. He was satisfied to be the understudy to Moses, his spiritual mentor, leader, and friend. Joshua was content to follow Moses and do whatever Moses said or did. But then, abruptly, he learned that going solo with God was neither easy nor optional.

Neither is it an option for you!

Since it's not optional, what do you need to know to be prepared to go solo with God? What are you supposed to do when the time comes to separate from the spiritual coat tails of your spiritual mentor whom you've trusted and followed? If you have yet to go through this separation, is there anything you can do now, in the present, so the separation doesn't seem quite so abrupt?

### The Speed Bump: Going Solo With God

There was a time early in his life when Joshua was comfortable with his spiritual experience. However, it was Moses' relationship with God that he was comfortable with, not his.

For a long time, Joshua and the people of Israel followed Moses. Moses had a special connection to God. He received direction from God and then spoke God's message to the Israelites. The Israelites did not always agree with Moses, nor did they always listen and obey, but they understood that he had a special connection with God that they didn't possess.

Joshua never doubted Moses. He knew Moses had an intimate relationship with God. Joshua had firsthand experience of the encounters between God and Moses: he was at the foot of the mountain while Moses received the Ten Commandments; he saw the cloud of God descend on the mountain when Moses met with God; he knew what was hidden under the veil Moses wore.

Suddenly, everything changed for Joshua and the Israelites. Moses died, and the nation of Israel looked to Joshua for spiritual leadership and direction. Joshua could no longer hide under the "spiritual security blanket" of Moses. The death of Moses proved to be a major speed bump in Joshua's life. He now had to practice His own *Prayer Dialogue* with God.

### *God Is Speaking In The Speed Bump*

Does this feel familiar? Does Joshua's situation replicate something you've experienced? Has the time come for you to go solo with God? Are you ready to connect with God, developing your own personal relationship with Him? Are you ready to begin living out your own personal Prayer Dialogue and stop living as a bookmark in the pages of others?

*Are you ready to begin living out your own personal Prayer Dialogue and stop living as a book- mark in the pages of others?*

Joshua's transition to flying solo with God can teach us many lessons. First, let's study his background, which will lead us to his conversion in the Book of Joshua.

Joshua was second-in-command to Moses, who had been enlisted by God to lead the Israelites out Egypt. After the miraculous parting of the Red Sea, Moses led the people to Mount Sinai to receive further instructions. God told Moses and his leaders to climb the mountain of God, but only Moses was to approach God. There Moses received the Ten Commandments and heard again of the Promised Land that God was taking them.

Two years later, as the Israelites approached the land promised to them by God, Moses sent twelve spies ahead of them into the land, called Canaan, to explore and report back with their findings. The majority report was discouraging. Ten of the spies recommended that Moses not lead the people into the land because it was full of giants who, the spies feared, would surely enslave them as the Egyptians had. Joshua and Caleb, the two dissenters, fully believed the Israelites could conquer the inhabitants and possess the land of Canaan as their land promised by God.

Moses adopted the negative majority report, thus revealing a lack of faith and trust in God. God spoke and told Moses that his refusal to go where He had instructed would result in the nation of Israel wandering for another 38 years in the desert, where the unbelieving generation would die in the wilderness. Moses and the Israelites of that generation had forfeited their right and privilege to enter the land God promised them.

The Israelite nation wandered in the wilderness for a total of 40 years. Before Moses died, God took him atop Mount Nebo to let him see the land that had been promised. Joshua and Caleb were the only adults of their generation to have survived the forty years in the wilderness—the only two who were permitted to enter into the Promise Land.

### How To Make The Most Of This Speed Bump

The leadership mantle of Moses was then passed on to Joshua after Moses' death. How did Joshua cope with this major change in his life? How did he make it over the speed bump and start going solo with God? I think you'll find the steps he took particularly helpful to you as you make a similar transition.

## Step 1: Expect God to Personally Guide You

When you go solo with God, He will not delegate your orientation session to one of His angels, assistants, or apprentices. God Himself will get personally involved. If you are willing to go solo with God, you will experience the very presence of God in your life.

Notice how this is dramatically shown in Joshua 1:1-5 (NASB):

> *"Now it came about after the death of Moses the servant of the LORD, that the LORD spoke to Joshua the son of Nun, Moses' servant, saying,* *² "Moses My servant is dead; now therefore arise, cross this Jordan, you and all this people, to the land which I am giving to them, to the sons of Israel. ³ "Every place on which the sole of your foot treads, I have given it to you, just as I spoke to Moses. ⁴ "From the wilderness and this Lebanon, even as far as the great river, the river Euphrates, all the land of the Hittites, and as far as the Great Sea toward the setting of the sun will be your territory.* *⁵ "No man will be able to stand before you all the days of your life. Just as I have been with Moses, I will be with you; I will not fail you or forsake you.' "*

God repeated this promise several times in the first chapter of Joshua. Time and time again He told Joshua that He would go with him and be with him.

When you go solo with God, you now have a personal connection with the God of the universe! He commits Himself to you and to be vitally involved in your life. In fact, that's why He sent His Son, Jesus. Because of Jesus, there is no longer a need to go through a priest or a holy man to converse or commune with God. Jesus has become humanity's mediator; He has invited all who are willing to come in faith and enter into an intimate relationship with God.

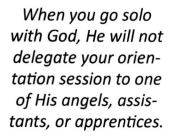

*When you go solo with God, He will not delegate your orientation session to one of His angels, assistants, or apprentices.*

Joshua was faced with a situation where the people recognized him as the practical choice to take Moses' place as their leader. Their loyalty to him was to be expected. But, remember, Joshua was a man who had ridden the coat tails of a spiritual giant; he had yet to go solo with God. As Joshua took his first step, God told him that His presence would be all he needed. God's call on Joshua was not to become a "Moses" clone. God simply wanted Joshua to respond with a personal commitment to follow Him.

Experiencing God's presence in your life has nothing to do with how gifted, talented, wise, or experienced you are. The bottom line is whether God is with you or not.

The danger in going solo with God is seeing God's presence as a passive presence. Even though you may acknowledge His presence, you still may feel like it's up to you to figure everything out. God knows how self-sufficient people tend to be. Unfortunately, that's why He will often have to wait until you fail before the promise of His presence makes any sense. God wants you to learn to trust Him and look to Him constantly.

This first step to going solo is so important: Know that God will be with you! His presence is essential because it will prompt you to make decisions based upon what He wants to do, what He can do, and what He says He will do. He doesn't want you to limit your life on the basis of what you think you can do or what you've seen somebody else do. This may sound like you are to ignore logical conclusions and limited resources when making decisions, but you are not. You need to count the cost of anything you are about to do. But never forget the "Presence of God" factor. He is always with you. Scripture says:

> *"Trust in the LORD with all your heart, and do not lean on your own understanding; in all your ways acknowledge Him and He will make your paths straight."* (Proverbs 3:5-6 NASB)

God's presence in any situation will significantly alter the plans of a man or woman. Oftentimes, your "religious" planning excludes the presence of God. You must be careful not to keep Him out.

Jesus had to remind His disciples of the importance of His presence prior to His ascension into Heaven. They were quite distraught that He was leaving them. Not understanding His purpose in leaving, they wanted Him to stay with them longer. Jesus assured them that after He ascended He would send the Holy Spirit, who would be with them always. It was also at this time when He reminded them of the mission of the church. He knew that these disciples would, like some of us in today's churches often do, conclude that the mission was something they could handle on their own after He left.

*Experiencing God's presence in your life has nothing to do with how gifted, talented, wise, or experienced you are.*

The promise of God's Holy Spirit was a reminder that the mission of the church was not something Jesus had delegated to the disciples. Rather, it was a declaration of what He was planning to do personally and that He was inviting them to join Him. Notice the very familiar Great Commission passage in Matthew 28:18-20:

> *"Then Jesus came near to them and said to them, 'All authority has been given to Me in Heaven and on Earth. Go, therefore, and make disciples of all the nations, baptizing them in the name of the Father, the Son, and the Holy Spirit, teaching them to observe everything I have commanded you. And remember, I am with you always, to the end of the age.' "*

In other words, Jesus said the task of the church was: "Introduce people to Me. I want them to connect with Me. I want them to go public with that connection through baptism, and then, once they connect, I want you to teach them the things that I have been teaching you." After He clearly described the mission, He added one very important phrase: *"And remember, I am with you always, to the end of the Age."*

*The promise of God's Holy Spirit was a reminder that the mission of the church was not something Jesus had delegated to the disciples.*

Going solo with God means you can expect God to personally guide you and accompany you. You are never going to be alone! You may feel like you are alone; you may even treat God like you are alone. But know that God will always be present when you decide to go solo with Him.

## Step 2: Live According to God's Instruction Manual.

Once you know and expect God to personally guide you as you go solo with Him, you need to live according to God's instruction manual—because your success will depend on it! Read Joshua 1:6-7 (NASB):

> *"Be strong and courageous, for you shall give this people possession of the land which I swore to their fathers to give them. ⁷ "Only be strong and very courageous; be careful to do according to all the law which Moses My servant commanded you; do not turn from it to the right or to the left, so that you may have success wherever you go."*

God assured Joshua that He wanted him to succeed! It was going to require strength and courage but, ultimately, Joshua's success depended on his commitment to do things as prescribed by God in "this book of instruction." (Joshua 1:8)

God's instruction manual is the Bible. God wanted Joshua— and He wants you—to read and apply the instruction of His manual to your life. Not only is it the secret to success (Joshua 1:8), but it will also help prevent you from making a lot of unnecessary and foolish mistakes.

The Bible talks about relationships, decision-making, and integrity. It talks about your future and goes into much detail about the uniqueness and value of your personality, personal gifts, and abilities. It describes what to do when you are angry, depressed, and lonely. Everything you will need to know in order to live the kind of successful life prescribed by God is found in His Word.

In fact, God guaranteed this success to Joshua if he prioritized and personalized the Scripture. Read Joshua 1:8:

> *"This book of the law shall not depart from your mouth, but you shall meditate on it day and night, so that you may be careful to do according to all that is written in it; for then you will make your way prosperous, and then you will have success."*

That is a promise from God! You are going to succeed and prosper in whatever you do if you choose to live life according to His instruction manual. But you must consult it on a regular basis. God says you need to go over it, *"day and night."*

God says you will succeed and prosper if you *daily* align your life with Scripture. You cannot expect these kinds of results if you search the Scriptures only when you are in trouble, need a job, have to make a major decision, or are sick. You must habitually and daily invest time reading and meditating on the Scriptures. As you do, God will use His Word to instruct, correct, and encourage you along the way.

God wants you to always have the Scriptures easily accessible for decision-making. To "recite it day and night" is to commit it to memory so that it can immediately influence your heart and mind. Memorizing Scripture passages will result in significant changes in your life. As you expose your mind to Scripture daily, memorize it, and retain it, you can expect it to shape your attitudes, affect your decisions, temper your emotions, and improve your relationships.

Are you still questioning the importance of committing the Bible to memory?" Read Joshua 1:6-7 again:

> *"Be strong and courageous, for you shall give this people possession of the land which I swore to their fathers to give them.* ⁷ *"Only be strong and very courageous; be careful to do according to all the law which Moses My servant commanded you; do not turn from it to the right or to the left, so that you may have success wherever you go."*

Twice in this passage, God told Joshua to be strong and courageous. Those are two very significant words. The word "strong" is the Hebrew word "kazak," which means "to fortify" or "to have a strong foundation." When God said to be strong, He was telling Joshua—and all future readers of His Word—to stand on something that will not collapse beneath them; it is not enough to simply feel confident or strong, but you must take your stand on something that will hold up under pressure. What will stand firm under you, never collapsing or giving way to pressure? God's Word! God's Word is and will always be that firm foundation that is true, reliable, and unchanging.

But look again at Joshua 1:6. God also says to be "courageous." The Hebrew for courageous in this verse is "amatz," which means, "determined and forward-moving." "Courageous" living means you are confidently looking forward and able to be decisive. In this passage, the term, "amatz," is applied in relationship to "kazak." Therefore, the confidence to move forward is based upon the assurance that you are leaping from an immovable and firm foundation.

When you combine "courage" with "strength," you actually have the two components of Biblical faith as defined in Hebrews 11:1 (KJV): *"Now faith is the substance of things hoped for, the evidence of things not seen."* Faith is the "reality (or substance) of what is hoped for." This is the equivalent of the word "kazak" or "strength from a firm foundation." God's Word is that upon which you stand.

Faith is also "the proof (or evidence) of what is not seen." This is similar to "amatz" or courage that leads to action. Faith is knowing, with assurance, the truth of God's Word and then acting in obedience to it. There are going to be times when you have to take some risks. The person who is not "courageous" will always come up with an excuse not to trust God. But whenever God tells you to do something through His Word, you can know that He is under obligation to provide the resources you will need and empower you to do it.

That is why God told Joshua to be courageous. His Word is the firm and stable foundation that you can stake your life on. God wants you to be strong and courageous. He wants you to know the truth of the Bible so well that you act courageously on it. You can only do this if you take the time to study, memorize, and apply it.

### Step 3: Don't Get Ahead of God

Read again the first two verses of Joshua 1 (NIV):

> *After the death of Moses the servant of the LORD, the LORD said to Joshua son of Nun, Moses' aide: ² "Moses my servant is dead. Now then, you and all these people, get ready to cross the Jordan River into the land I am about to give to them—to the Israelites.*

Notice that God did not say, "You and all the people should cross the Jordan River right now." He instructed them to prepare to cross over.

This instruction from God to prepare is puzzling. The Israelites had been wandering in the desert for 40 years. How much more "preparing" did they need to do? But that is the point. Oftentimes your feelings will mislead you into thinking that you are ready to follow God's lead when you really are not ready. God, in His infinite knowledge, knows when you are ready to accomplish His plans, and He will let you know when it's time to move.

Read Joshua 1:10-12:

> *"Then Joshua commanded the officers of the people, saying, "Pass through the midst of the camp and command the people," saying, "Prepare provisions for yourselves, for within three days you are to cross this Jordan, to go in to possess the land which the LORD your God is giving you, to possess it."'*

48

God instructed Joshua that in three days the people will be crossing over the Jordan into the Promised Land. The people are to get their affairs in order, pack their possessions, and prepare their families. The three-day wait wasn't a time to be idle but rather to proactively prepare.

God's timing is always perfect. If God tells you to wait, it is for a specific reason. Waiting is never intended to be a waste of time. There are always things yet to be learned or done while you wait to move forward.

So how do you effectively wait on God? Let's look at what Joshua did:

> *"Then Joshua the son of Nun sent two men as spies secretly from Shittim, saying, "Go, view the land, especially Jericho." So they went and came into the house of a harlot whose name was Rahab, and lodged there."* (Joshua 2:1 NASB).

Why did Joshua send the spies secretly? Do you remember what happened the last time spies were sent into the Promised Land? Very publicly, Moses sent twelve spies into Canaan, and they returned with the opinion that the people should not enter the land at that time. Joshua never forgot that tragic lesson. This time, there would be no debate regarding whether they enter the Promised Land; that had already been decided. In three days the Israelites were going to cross the Jordan River, enter into Canaan, and take possession of the city of Jericho. Joshua was using God's mandated waiting period to gather information and prepare for what was ahead. Joshua was effectively and proactively waiting on God's timing.

*Waiting on God is never an idle time. In fact, seeking God requires a lot of concentration and alertness.*

When you are waiting, seek God. Pursue Him! Go after Him! Tell Him that you want to know Him more. Waiting on God is never an idle time. In fact, seeking God requires a lot of concentration and alertness. Psalm 130:6 says, *"I wait for the Lord more than watchmen for the morning, more than watchmen for the morning."*

What does a watchman do? A watchman is always on alert and constantly watching for any sign of the enemy. He sits at his post at night, staring intently into the darkness for any indication of a sneak attack or ambush. His job isn't to sit back and relax. His job is to be extremely attentive—always pacing the wall, looking for anything unusual, and listening for abnormal sounds. When the sun comes up, a watchman is relieved and can finally relax as he accomplished his mission.

Waiting on God is very similar to the activity of a watchman. During times of waiting, stay focused and pay attention to any sign or fingerprint of God—He is going to be speaking to you, and you don't want to miss a single word. If you are not alert, unlike a watchman, you will miss the message when it comes. God wants you to be proactive while you are waiting in order to teach you things about future decisions you will have to make. Bottom line: don't get ahead of God; His timing is always perfect!

### Step 4: Keep Telling Others What God Has Done in Your Life.

If you have already entered into a redeemed relationship with Jesus, your mission is to tell other people about Him. God wants people to know that He loves them and that they can personally know Him. Unfortunately, so many people do not even have a clue concerning God's love and purpose! Many wonder, "Where is God? All I see is suffering, wars, and evil." A person who is going solo with God is positioned perfectly to help others connect with Jesus.

Read Joshua 3:7-8:

*Now the LORD said to Joshua, "This day I will*
*begin to exalt you in the sight of all Israel, that*
*they may know that just as I have been with*
*Moses, I will be with you.*
*⁸ "You shall, moreover, command the priests who*
*are carrying the ark of the covenant, saying,*
*'When you come to the edge of the waters of*
*the Jordan, you shall stand still in the Jordan." ' "*

The waiting period of three days elapsed, and it was time for the people to move into the Promised Land. But before the Israelites marched upon Jericho, God wanted to do something else. God instructed the priests to carry the Ark of the Covenant to the edge of the Jordan River ahead of the people. He next told Joshua to command the priests to go into the Jordan River with the Ark of the Covenant.

So Joshua obeyed God and commanded the priests to walk into the river. As they stepped in, the water receded on either side, just as it had with the Red Sea when they were leaving Egypt with Moses! The water stopped upstream with an invisible barrier and the downstream flow was non-existent. The ground beneath their feet became dry. There was not even a trace of water or mud!

The entire Israelite nation crossed the Jordan River, just like the previous generation had done at the Red Sea. When they got to the other side, God instructed Joshua to pick twelve men, one from each tribe of Israel, and have them select a stone from the riverbed and carry it with them to their place of encampment. The twelve men carried their stones to the place called Gilgal.

That brings us to Joshua 4:19-24:

*"Now the people came up from the Jordan on*
*the tenth of the first month and camped at Gilgal*
*on the eastern edge of Jericho. ²⁰ Those twelve*

*stones which they had taken from the Jordan, Joshua set up at Gilgal. <sup>21</sup> He said to the sons of Israel, "When your children ask their fathers in time to come, saying, 'What are these stones?' <sup>22</sup> then you shall inform your children, saying, 'Israel crossed this Jordan on dry ground.'*
*<sup>23</sup> "For the LORD your God dried up the waters of the Jordan before you until you had crossed, just as the LORD your God had done to the Red Sea, which He dried up before us until we had crossed; <sup>24</sup> that all the peoples of the earth may know that the hand of the LORD is mighty, so that you may fear the LORD your God forever' "*

God accomplished all of these things in order to construct a foundation for faith and credibility with the next generation of Israelites. He purposefully coupled this miracle to the miracles performed under their former leader, Moses, as a way to encourage the Israelites that He would be with them as He had been with Moses. It was as if God were saying, "What I did with Moses, I can do again. Growing up, you heard your parents talk about what I did to liberate them from the Egyptians. Now I want you to experience and see for yourselves what I can do."

The Israelites set up the boulders as a reminder to themselves and other generations of just how great God was. The boulders were intended to prompt future generations to ask their significance. The people then would be able to explain what God did and just how mighty He was.

That's what God wants you to do. Many people don't know what God has done in the past, nor are they aware that God is alive and active today. It is so important that you construct markers in your life that prompt conversations about the greatness of God.

Life on Earth is short. If you have entered into and cultivated a relationship with Christ, you have so much to look forward to!

However, you are surrounded by friends, neighbors, and family members who have not yet experienced God personally. You have to show them Christ's love—now!

Show the people in your life the boulders that mark your experiences with God. Show them what God has been doing in your life. Share with them! Don't allow your Christian life to remain a secret.

If you just tell others religious facts and wag your finger at them in condemnation when they don't live like you do, they will probably ignore you. But if you tell them what God has done and is doing in your life, they will listen. That is why you dare not tolerate anything less than an intimate and growing relationship with God—a prayer dialogue. When you go solo with God, you will gain the respect of those with whom you share the Good News about Jesus. This flows right into the fifth step of going solo with God.

## Step 5: Identify Yourself as a Follower of Jesus Christ

God has not called you to lead a secret Christian life. His calling on your life is to be very public. But that doesn't mean you need to be obnoxious or abrasively confrontational. God wants you to communicate to others what He has done in your life with "gentleness and respect" (1 Peter 3:15-16). If you have been radically changed by God, you will find yourself compelled to share that change with others. It's only natural to want to share with others what you have personally experienced yourself.

The public nature of God's calling of a person is demonstrated by the Israelites before they were allowed by God to fight against Jericho. God told Joshua there was one thing they needed to take care of before they went any further. This conversation begins in Joshua 5:2:

> *"At that time the Lord said to Joshua, 'Make for yourself flint knives and circumcise again the sons of Israel the second time.' "*

What? Why would God give this command now? Why is this so important? The answer is found in verses 4 and 5:

> *"This is the reason why Joshua circumcised them: all the people who came out of Egypt who were males, all the men of war, died in the wilderness along the way after they came out of Egypt. ⁵ For all the people who came out were circumcised, but all the people who were born in the wilderness along the way as they came out of Egypt had not been circumcised."*

God wanted to make sure that the men who entered the Promised Land bore the mark of their covenant with God: circumcision. Their obedience would be evidence of their willingness to go public with their relationship with God.

Nothing has changed since the time of Joshua. It is still important to God that His people be publicly identified with Him. In the Old Testament, the mark was circumcision. However, in the New Testament and now, in the Church Age, that mark is baptism.

*God has not called you to lead a secret Christian life. His calling on your life is to be very public.*

The Bible says that whenever you commit your life to Christ, you need to go public with your new relationship with God by baptism. Baptism is your way of personally identifying with Jesus, who died and was resurrected from the dead. When a person is immersed in baptismal waters it is a symbol of identification with the death, burial, and resurrection of Christ.

When a person gets baptized, he or she is saying, "I have placed my faith in Jesus, the One who died and rose from the dead for me." It is a personal testimony to all.

Shortly after Jesus ascended into Heaven, there was the annual Feast of Pentecost. Thousands of people came to Jerusalem for the festivities. In Acts 2 it is recorded that Jesus' disciples were in a small room, huddled together praying and waiting. Suddenly, the Spirit of God descended upon them. Simon Peter went outside to where all the people were gathered and began to preach. He told them about Jesus and the significance of His death and resurrection. The people came under conviction, understanding that a personal relationship with God was something that could be realized. They were now able to go solo with God.

These people wondered what they should do next. Peter answered their question:

> *"When they heard this, they were pierced to the heart and said to Peter and the rest of the apostles: 'Brothers, what must we do?' 'Repent,' Peter said to them, 'and be baptized, each of you, in the name of Jesus the Messiah for the forgiveness of your sins, and you will receive the gift of the Holy Spirit.' ... So those who accepted his message were baptized, and that day about 3,000 people were added to them."* (Acts 2:37-38, 41)

Amazing! Three thousand people repented of their sin, went solo with God, and were baptized immediately. They understood the public nature of this new commitment and relationship. Going solo with God is always very personal but also intended by God to be very public.

*Going solo with God is always very personal but also intended by God to be very public.*

If you would like to personally connect with God, simply respond like the three thousand people did when Peter spoke to them. He first said to "repent." To repent simply means to admit that you have sinned against God and are now humbly choosing to turn to God and accept His gift of forgiveness. You realize that you don't have any right to even talk to God about this but you understand that you can approach God on the basis of what Jesus did on the cross. Once you do that, God forgives you, adopts you into His family, and sends His Spirit as His seal of ownership. It is then that you'll want to schedule a time with your pastor to be baptized. Going solo with God means that you will take this kind of initiative.

## Step 6: Expect Change as You Follow God

I am just like everybody else when it comes to change: I don't like it. We all tend to get comfortable right where we are. However, when you go solo with God, there are going to be all sorts of changes. God will transform you, adjust your circumstances, and change your friends. He will change everything!

Going solo with God demands change, and you must be flexible and grow with the changes. Notice what happens to Joshua and the Israelites in Chapter 5:

> *"While the sons of Israel camped at Gilgal they observed the Passover on the evening of the fourteenth day of the month on the desert plains of Jericho. ¹¹ On the day after the Passover, on that very day, they ate some of the produce of the land, unleavened cakes and parched grain. ¹² The manna ceased on the day after they had eaten some of the produce of the land, so that the sons of Israel no longer had manna, but they ate some of the yield of the land of Canaan during that year."* (Joshua 5:10-12)

Did you catch that? While the Israelites were in the desert, God had continued to give them manna ... for forty years! Every morning (except for the Sabbath) they collected the manna to eat—enough for the entire day. I'm sure the Israelites had gotten quite proficient in their manna-collecting and manna-cooking habits. They likely had a collection of recipes devoted to preparing manna. God used it to sustain and satisfy them during those many years in the wilderness. They had come to expect it. In fact, the new generation of Israelites that went into the Promised Land could hardly remember a "pre-manna" time. Then God told them there would be no more manna.

Can you imagine their anxiety? These people had not eaten anything other than manna, and an occasional quail, for forty years. You can almost envision some of the conversations that ensued: "I have my great-grandmother's recipe for Manna-burgers. Now what will I eat?" or "I like manna! I don't want to eat grapes!" This was a radical change for them; they were comfortable and familiar with the way things were. Some of them even wondered aloud why God would curse them in this way.

This response might seem overly dramatic to you right now, but it's really not much different from how most everybody responds to change. When God brings about changes in your life, are you often quick to misunderstand? Do you grumble and complain? Do you view the change as a curse? It's easy to view change as a negative thing. You may even conclude that changes are occurring because God has distanced Himself from you. However, this couldn't be farther from the truth.

*While you may not like the immediate consequences of change, you will be pleasantly surprised by the long-term results of change.*

God changes things for your best! When you connect with Christ, He changes everything. When you embrace these changes, it will produce an uncommon joy, supernatural peace, and renewed hope deep within you. Those are just a few of the ways Christ will make a difference in your life. While you may not like the immediate consequences of change, you will be pleasantly surprised by the long-term results of change. When you go solo with God, you can expect the following specific changes:

- **The way you treat others**: When you connect with Christ, you are going to treat others with compassion and respect. Love and forgiveness will be frequently demonstrated.
- **Your sensitivity to sin**: No longer will you be able to just shrug off sin as a simple mistake. Sin will begin to bother you because you know that you have settled for less than God's best.
- **Your circumstances**: You will notice changes in your circumstances because of God.
- **Your circle of friends**: Your friends will change. God plans to use new people in your life to encourage you and help shape you into the person God created you to be.
- **Your passion to know God**: You will find you have an unquenchable thirst to know Him. It's no longer enough to read about Him or hear others talk about Him. You'll want to know Him personally and intimately.
- **Your desire to live for Him**: You realize that you were created for a purpose. You will find yourself seeking to know that purpose and live it out.
- **The way you "do" church**: Attending a church service will not be enough for you anymore. You will also want to grow deeper and serve others. "Church" will become the time when the body of Christ is working together to glorify God. This will occur during times of worship but far more in times of ministry together.

While you may not necessarily like the changes, they are necessary. God's desire is to connect with you. This will requires change—it will require that *you* change. It is inevitable ... God is going to take your manna away.

Finally, as you go solo with God, be sure to pay attention to additional speed bumps like the one Joshua experienced below—also known as a "Holy Ground" experience.

### Step 7: Don't Ignore "Holy Ground" Experiences

Discover what happened next to Joshua:

> *"Now it came about when Joshua was by Jericho, that he lifted up his eyes and looked, and behold, a man was standing opposite him with his sword drawn in his hand, and Joshua went to him and said to him, "Are you for us or for our adversaries?"* ¹⁴ *He said, "No; rather I indeed come now as captain of the host of the LORD." And Joshua fell on his face to the earth, and bowed down, and said to him, "What has my lord to say to his servant?"* ¹⁵ *The captain of the LORD'S host said to Joshua, "Remove your sandals from your feet, for the place where you are standing is holy." And Joshua did so."* (Joshua 5:13-15 NASB)

Joshua wandered around, away from the campfire, thinking what he might do next. He thought through the strategy for invading of Jericho when suddenly he looked up and saw a daunting figure in front of him with sword drawn! His immediate reaction was to find out if this was a friend or foe. The man told Joshua he was neither for, nor against him. Instead, he confronted Joshua with the need to choose a side. Joshua immediately fell to his face and worshipped him.

What happened next was very interesting. God told Joshua to take off his shoes because he was standing on holy ground.

This same kind of "holy ground" experience is recorded many times in Scripture. It happened to Moses at the burning bush; it happened to Peter, James, and John at the Mount of Transfiguration. It also happens today: sometimes during a church service; other times while at home, on the job, or at school. You can expect it to happen whenever you have a solo encounter with God.

A holy ground experience brings you face-to-face with the Presence of God. It not only transforms ordinary dirt into "holy ground" but also changes and transforms you and your life. A holy ground experience transforms an ordinary church service into an experience with God. It changes a devotional moment into an intimate encounter with God. When you go solo with God, you can expect "holy ground" experiences similar to Joshua. Notice the following characteristics.

- *A holy ground experience usually takes you by surprise.* You may not be expecting it when it happens—Joshua wasn't expecting it—but God's timing is always perfect. You can't rush it or predict it. All you can do is accept it when He interrupts.
- *A holy ground experience is intended to refocus your attention on Jesus Christ.* In Joshua's case, he asked the man which side He is on. The man replied, "Neither. I have now come as commander of the Lord's army." God changed the focus from a commitment of the task at hand to a renewed loyalty to the Lord Himself. Joshua was forced to momentarily divert his attention from the battle of Jericho to his allegiance and loyalty to the Lord God Almighty.
- *A holy ground experience will force you to re-examine your devotion to God.* That is the point of a "holy ground" experience. God wants to make sure you are focused on Him, not His assignment. Your relationship

60

with Him will then become the motivation and source of strength and wisdom to accomplish His assignment.

- ***A holy ground experience transforms the routine into the supernatural.*** God plans to turn your ordinary experiences into extraordinary ones. His plan requires His supernatural power. It will require your admission of inadequacy and dependence of His adequacy. His desire is to break you of you habitual tendency to live according to your own resources and personal strength. The holy ground experience is intended to highlight the fingerprints of God, not the accomplishments of men.
- ***A holy ground experience requires a personal response.*** Joshua responded to the commander of the Lord's army in a personal way: *"Joshua bowed with his face to the ground in worship"* (Joshua 5:14). He displayed humility and awe of God. Joshua recognized he was experiencing something different, and he submitted himself completely to God and demonstrated a wholehearted desire and readiness to serve Him.
- ***A holy ground experience requires vulnerability and reverence to God.*** God commanded Joshua to take off his sandals. As a soldier, this probably seemed odd to Joshua, because he needed to be ready to move at a moment's notice. If he removed his shoes, he would become vulnerable. But this is exactly what God wants—for you to become vulnerable to Him!

## *How Will You Respond?*

It's time to take God seriously when He declares the ground where you are standing as "holy." He wants you to become vulnerable and to revere Him. This can only happen when you go solo with God. It is irrelevant whether or not He is literally asking you to remove the shoes from our feet. God wants to know: Are you willing to do whatever it is He asks you to do?

Are you interested in having a "holy ground" experience, or are you going to remain guarded and shielded?

Oftentimes, in my study at work, I will take my shoes off in order to remind myself that I am not here just to accomplish a list of tasks. Instead, I am here to seek the face of God.

Responding to God's presence looks different for each individual. If you have never initiated a relationship with Him by asking Jesus to come into your life, you need to do that first. You need to come to Him asking for forgiveness and ask Him to come into your life. Commit yourself to Him and make yourself completely vulnerable before Him.

If you have already committed your life to Christ but have never been baptized, you need to go public in your relationship with Him. Before you can fully experience God's holy ground, you must become submissive and vulnerable before Him.

You may already have entered into that personal relationship with Jesus and have been baptized. However, you have yet to go solo with Him. Take the steps, like Joshua, to go solo with God and begin your own *Prayer Dialogue*. Going solo led Joshua to a "holy ground" experience with God. It will lead you, as well, to your own "holy ground" experience. God says, "Take your shoes off and kneel before Me. This is holy ground. Listen to Me."

It's time to get serious. Are you ready to go solo with God?

## QUESTIONS FOR PERSONAL EVALUATION AND DISCUSSION:

1. Are you allowing self-righteousness (man-made efforts) to define your relationship with God or are you resting in an intimate relationship with him based on HIS righteousness?
2. How do you think you can cooperate with God in His plan for your personal faith journey?
3. Going solo with God requires one to go public with their faith. Reflecting on Acts 2:37-38 and 41; how

can you personally apply the lessons demonstrated by the growth and public faith shown by Peter and the apostles?

**PRAYER:**

*Heavenly Father, help me to respond to You in a way that would honor You. Lord, it is so easy for me to become so busy and to rush You. God, I want to get up close and personal with You and am willing to remove my shoes before walking into Your Presence. Help me to remove my own hindrances in order to approach You with vulnerability like never before. God, once I am at your feet, teach me the things You desperately want me to know, so that I'll never be the same again.*

# JOSHUA

## SPEED BUMPS

- The death of Moses
- Instructions to lead the people of God into the Promised Land
- Confrontation of the Commander of Lord of Hosts before Jericho

---

## WHAT IS NECESSARY TO CHANGE YOUR PRAYER MONOLOGUE INTO A PRAYER DIALOGUE?

Go Solo with God

*Chapter 4*

# FIGHTING WITH GOD: JACOB

A few years ago, I travelled to Zimbabwe on a church mission trip. It was an amazing trip. The economic and political circumstances in that country were desperate and prompted a national longing for radical change. This need for and openness to change created an acute awareness of their personal spiritual condition. In less than a week, more than 10,000 people responded to our daily invitation to place their faith in Jesus Christ as their personal Lord and Savior. It was a miraculous answer to our prayers.

On the final day of our trip we took a break and visited a wild game preserve populated with zebras, elephants, giraffes, and lions. The animals roamed freely on this preserve. Guides escorted us as we rode in Jeeps and on horses throughout the preserve, and we were able to get very close to the animals ... including young lions!

This preserve was known for its *"Walk With The Lions."* For those who were interested—and we certainly were—an opportunity to walk with lions occurred twice a day. These particular lions had grown up on the preserve and were full size, but only thirteen or fourteen months old.

Before we walked with the lions the guides met with us and taught us how to avoid becoming a lion's next meal or wrestling partner. We were taught to blend in with two of the lions as we walked throughout the African terrain. We learned how to think and act like a lion.

The guides explained that lions often spar with other lions for the right to be leader–the Alpha-Male. As the lions age, it is normal that they test the Alpha-Male by first getting eye contact with him. Obviously, that explains why we were told never to make eye contact with a lion. Eye contact is considered the beginning of a challenge by a lion and usually leads to a combative encounter. Long walking sticks were issued to each of us to distract the lion if he seemed a little too interested in us. Tapping the ground with a stick was an effective way of interrupting the eye contact and stopping a possible physical altercation. Looking back at this, I now find myself thinking, "What was I thinking?!"

If we acted inappropriately, like run or stare, we would have been the ones to lose—not the lions. Humans will never win a wrestling match with a full-grown lion fully equipped with sharp claws and long teeth. Even if they are just playing, we are going to get hurt! At approximately 16 months old, the male lions begin challenging other lions in order to become the Alpha Male. However, when one lion dominates in a fight and becomes the Alpha Male, it is merely a temporary position until challenged again.

### *The Speed Bump: Fighting With God*

Humans are not very different from the male lion. We tend to be self-centered and want to be in charge. It's only when we think we can't control our circumstances that we are willing to give up control … but rarely without a fight. We act like we believe we are the Alpha-Male in our relationship with God. This always proves to be problematic and leads to prayer monologues rather than prayer dialogues. We'd rather tell God

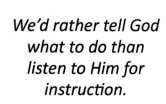

*We'd rather tell God what to do than listen to Him for instruction.*

what to do than listen to Him for instruction. When you and I go down this road it always leads to a fight with God. The fight then becomes a speed bump that God uses to transform our prayer monologue into a prayer dialogue. Let's look at man named Jacob who had such an encounter with God.

### *God Is Speaking In The Speed Bump*

Jacob was a man who was not afraid to fight. His father was Isaac, the son of Abraham; and his twin brother was Esau. When Jacob and Esau were born, Esau came out first with Jacob hanging onto his heel. In Hebrew, the name Jacob literally means, *"supplanter: one who wrongfully or illegally seizes and holds the place of another."* From the very beginning, Jacob was literally on the heels of his older brother, as if to say: "Oh no, you don't … you are not getting out before me! If I were stronger, I'd pull you back and get out first!" Being second-born did not stop Jacob from pursuing the role of Alpha-Male. Jacob always looked for ways to take what was not his.

Jacob exerted his desire to "supplant" on one particular occasion when his brother Esau was at his weakest. Esau had been hunting and was really hungry. He returned home and found Jacob, who was a good cook, preparing a deliciously smelling stew. Esau asked for a taste. Jacob replied, "On one condition: give me your birthright!" Esau, famished from a day of arduous hunting, said: "What good is my birthright if am I dead from starvation? Take it!" Jacob manipulated the situation and stole Esau's birthright. After realizing what had been done, Esau resented Jacob for stealing what was naturally and rightfully his and from that day forward looked for a way to retaliate.

When it became clear to Jacob and Esau's father, Isaac, that he was about to die he called for Esau, the eldest son. Esau met with his father, who told him to go on a hunt, prepare the kill, and bring the food to him so that he may give Esau his blessing. The drama gets complicated when we find out that Esau's mother, Rebekah, overheard the conversation between Isaac and Esau. Since Jacob was her favorite son, Rebekah wanted Jacob to receive the blessing. So she told Jacob to go into his father's tent and pretend to be Esau. Since Isaac was old and could not see very well, she believed that Jacob could fool Isaac by dressing him with animal hides and Esau's clothing. So, as soon as Jacob could prepare a dish he entered Isaac's tent masquerading as Esau. Isaac was suspicious and questioned Jacob about his identity. He was a bit confused by the sound of Jacob's voice.

After touching and smelling him, though, Isaac was fooled into believing that Jacob was Esau. He then ate the food and blessed Jacob with the firstborn blessing. Once again, Jacob the "supplanter," manipulated his own father into giving him what lawfully and rightfully belonged to his brother.

A little later, Esau ran into his father's tent after returning from the hunt. It was at that moment that Isaac realized what had happen. Outraged, Esau vowed to kill Jacob once his father died. Jacob's mother, fearful of losing her son, told him to flee to the country of his Uncle Laban. Jacob hoped time would diminish Esau's anger, so he decided his mother's idea was best and ended up living with Laban in the distant land of Haran for twenty-one years.

While living with his uncle's family in Haran, Jacob was introduced to Laban's two daughters: Leah, the older, and Rachel, the younger. Although it is customary for the older daughter to marry first, Jacob fell in love with Rachel, the more beautiful of the two women. Jacob offered to work for Laban for seven years in exchange for Rachel's hand in marriage. After working diligently for seven years, Laban tricked Jacob into marrying Leah, the older daughter. Feeling deceived, Jacob confronted Laban, who eventually told him that he would give Rachel to Jacob in marriage after another seven years of labor. After working an additional seven years Jacob was permitted to marry Rachel. After a total of twenty-one years, Jacob decided to move back home, bringing along all of his wives, children, and possessions accumulated over the past two decades.

Now that you are familiar with the background of Jacob and Esau's relationship let's look further to see what happened next. Let's read Genesis 32:1-32:

> "Now as Jacob went on his way, the angels of God met him. ² Jacob said when he saw them, "This is God's camp." So he named that place Mahanaim. ³ Then Jacob sent messengers before him to his brother Esau in the land of Seir, the country of Edom. ⁴ He also commanded them saying, "Thus you shall say to my lord Esau: 'Thus says your servant Jacob, "I have sojourned with Laban, and stayed until now; ⁵ I have oxen and donkeys and flocks and male and female servants; and I have sent to tell my lord, that I may find favor in your sight."'" ⁶ The messengers returned to Jacob, saying, "We came to your brother Esau, and furthermore he is coming to meet you, and four hundred men are with him." ⁷ Then Jacob was greatly afraid and distressed; and he divided the people who were with him, and the flocks and the herds and the camels, into two companies; ⁸ for he said, "If Esau comes to the one company and attacks it, then the company which is left will escape." ⁹ Jacob said, "O God of my father Abraham and God of my father Isaac, O LORD, who said to me, 'Return to your country and to your relatives, and I will prosper you,' ¹⁰ I am unworthy of all the lovingkindness and of all the faithfulness which You have shown to Your servant; for with my staff only I crossed this Jordan, and now I have become two companies. ¹¹ "Deliver me, I pray, from the hand of my brother, from the hand of Esau; for I fear him, that he will come and attack me and the mothers with the

children. ¹² "For You said, 'I will surely prosper you and make your descendants as the sand of the sea, which is too great to be numbered.'" ¹³ So he spent the night there. Then he selected from what he had with him a present for his brother Esau: ¹⁴ two hundred female goats and twenty male goats, two hundred ewes and twenty rams, ¹⁵ thirty milking camels and their colts, forty cows and ten bulls, twenty female donkeys and ten male donkeys. ¹⁶ He delivered them into the hand of his servants, every drove by itself, and said to his servants, "Pass on before me, and put a space between droves." ¹⁷ He commanded the one in front, saying, "When my brother Esau meets you and asks you, saying, 'To whom do you belong, and where are you going, and to whom do these animals in front of you belong?' ¹⁸ then you shall say, 'These belong to your servant Jacob; it is a present sent to my lord Esau. And behold, he also is behind us.'" ¹⁹ Then he commanded also the second and the third, and all those who followed the droves, saying, "After this manner you shall speak to Esau when you find him; ²⁰ and you shall say, 'Behold, your servant Jacob also is behind us.'" For he said, "I will appease him with the present that goes before me. Then afterward I will see his face; perhaps he will accept me." ²¹ So the present passed on before him, while he himself spent that night in the camp. ²² Now he arose that same night and took his two wives and his two maids and his eleven children, and crossed the ford of the Jabbok. ²³ He took them and sent them across the stream. And he sent across whatever he had. ²⁴ Then Jacob was left alone, and a man wrestled with him until daybreak. ²⁵

*When he saw that he had not prevailed against him, he touched the socket of his thigh; so the socket of Jacob's thigh was dislocated while he wrestled with him. <sup>26</sup> Then he said, "Let me go, for the dawn is breaking." But he said, "I will not let you go unless you bless me." <sup>27</sup> So he said to him, "What is your name?" And he said, "Jacob." <sup>28</sup> He said, "Your name shall no longer be Jacob, but Israel; for you have striven with God and with men and have prevailed." <sup>29</sup> Then Jacob asked him and said, "Please tell me your name." But he said, "Why is it that you ask my name?" And he blessed him there. <sup>30</sup> So Jacob named the place Peniel, for he said, "I have seen God face to face, yet my life has been preserved." <sup>31</sup> Now the sun rose upon him just as he crossed over Penuel, and he was limping on his thigh. <sup>32</sup> Therefore, to this day the sons of Israel do not eat the sinew of the hip which is on the socket of the thigh, because he touched the socket of Jacob's thigh in the sinew of the hip."*

This is a perfect illustration of a man who is used to being in charge of every facet of his life. He even fought for control in his relationship with God. Jacob's communication with God was one sided, a monologue. He was determined to work out his problems his own way.

Little did he know that his arrogant lifestyle would provoke a fight with God. Jacob would attempt to quickly win this fight while God chose to use the fight as a speed bump that would slow him down long enough to recognize the God he was fighting. When He finally realized he was fighting God, he knew he had only two options: submit to Him or blindly keep fighting until he had nothing left to fight with.

## Characteristics of a Fight with God

Nobody wants to admit that they are fighting with God. But the truth is that anytime you choose your ways over God's ways, you are picking a fight with Him. In fact, your persistent effort to resist Him is evidence that you really don't know God. The human heart is combative and selfish by nature. It is self-centered and self-serving. This has been the case since the Garden episode with Adam and Eve. Sin corrupted the relationship man was intended to have with God from the beginning. Since that time you, by nature, fight to maintain or gain control.

> *Anytime you choose your ways over God's ways, you are picking a fight with Him.*

But since God still loves you, He has chosen to use your inclination to fight as a vehicle to introduce you to His power, grace, and mercy. Every time you choose to fight with God, you become more aware of your inability to control Him. God's desire is that you give up control of your life, give it to Him, and follow Him. The speed bump that looks like a wrestling match with God is intended to result in a Prayer Dialogue that reflects and encourages greater intimacy with a God who created and loves you.

It is extremely important that you slow down at this speed bump and learn the lesson God is trying to teach you. This chapter is especially for you who constantly find yourself in a fight with God. Notice below the characteristics of a fight with God. I think you'll be able to identify with these.

### 1. You pick a fight with God whenever you put God in second place.

In Genesis 32 we clearly see Jacob's plans. He had all his ducks in a row. But they did not include God. Whenever you proceed without God, you are asking for a fight! Your plans and decisions say to God: "I don't need you! I have my own agenda." You might not be so brazen to say those words to God but that's what your plans without God loudly proclaim.

The prophet Isaiah spoke about the absurdity of living life and making plans without God.

> "Woe to those who deeply hide their plans from the LORD, and whose deeds are done in a dark place, and they say, "Who sees us?" or "Who knows us?" 16 You turn things around! Shall the potter be considered as equal with the clay, that what is made would say to its maker, "He did not make me"; or what is formed say to him who formed it, "He has no understanding"?" (Isaiah 29:15-16)

When you leave God out of your plans you are forgetting that He uniquely made you and has enabled you to be where you are at this moment. He is the One and Only God of the universe. He is the Creator of everything that is and He created you for Himself. In fact, He uniquely created you in His own image. He has creatively made men and women with the capacity and ability to know Him and relate to Him intimately. Usurping control from God in the planning and living of your life is to try and thwart God's plan for your life. God does not take this lightly.

In the Sermon on the Mount, Jesus talked about how a relationship with God works. He said to, "Seek first the Kingdom of God and His righteousness, and all these things will be added to you" (Matthew 6:33). What "things" is Jesus talking about? It includes the necessities of life. It includes everything you will ever need. It includes those things that you don't think God would want to deal with. The message is clear. God wants you to put Him first, above everything else. Once your priorities are set, with God being first, you position yourself to know

Him intimately. Putting God first is the first step toward transforming a prayer monologue into a prayer dialogue.

## 2. Your fight with God can only be avoided temporarily.

Some of you reading this book can't think of a time when you've actually fought with God. Perhaps it is because you are running from God. If so, eventually you'll run out of gas, get tired and collapse. Just know, once you slow down, the fight will begin.

Genesis 32:24 says, *"Jacob was left alone."* Jacob had made all the preparations to meet with Esau by dividing his family, herds, and possessions, but still he was left alone. The fight with God began here because Jacob could not run anymore.

You may be so busy running from God that you don't even realize you are resisting Him. The moment things get quiet you'll realize you've stepped into the ring with God. As long as you continue running at the pace you're running, you may feel like things are just fine. However, in reality, you are just delaying the inevitable, a fight with God.

Jonah experienced this firsthand:

> *"The word of the LORD came to Jonah the son of Amittai saying, ² "Arise, go to Nineveh the great city and cry against it, for their wickedness has come up before Me." ³ But Jonah rose up to flee to Tarshish from the presence of the LORD. So he went down to Joppa, found a ship which was going to Tarshish, paid the fare and went down into it to go with them to Tarshish from the presence of the LORD." (Jonah 1:1-3 NASB).*

God had initiated a prayer dialogue with Jonah to include him in God's plans for the city of Ninevah. Jonah, however, rejected God's plan, turned prayer into a monologue and ran to the seaport city of Joppa. He ran from God, so that he wouldn't have to face God any more.

You can run from God, but don't forget that God is patient. He will wait as long as it takes to get you to return to Him. In Jonah's case,

*"The LORD hurled a great wind on the sea and there was a great storm on the sea so that the ship was about to break up." (Jonah 1:4 NASB)*

You remember the rest of the story: Jonah was thrown overboard because all the sailors thought he was responsible for the storm that threatened all of their lives. Jonah was then swallowed by a big fish and remained there for three days. He ultimately cried out to God, re-established a prayer dialogue, and God delivered Him. God

> *You may be so busy running from God that you don't even realize you are resisting Him.*

then reminded him of the previous conversation concerning Nineveh. This time Jonah listened to God and did what He said to do.

The critical issue is whether you are going to follow your plan or God's plan. You will be embroiled in a fight as long as you resist God's plan. How much are you willing to lose and how far are you willing to run before finally submitting to the Lord? How many scars will be necessary before you turn to Him? How far from God will you run before you've run far enough?

### 3. <u>Expect God to start the fight.</u>

If you slow down and finally listen to God, will everything get better? Not without a struggle! Genesis 32:24 says, *"Jacob was left alone, and a man wrestled with him until daybreak."* We know that this man who wrestled with Jacob is God in the flesh. Hosea 12:3 says: *"In the womb he took his brother by the heel, and in his maturity he contended with God."*

This manifestation of God is called a *theophany*. Abraham (Genesis 18:16-21) and Joshua (Joshua 5:13-15) were privileged to encounter such a theophany and respectfully responded to God as He revealed Himself this way. But Jacob foolishly thought he could actually wrestle with God, and win. Flesh to flesh, God wrestled with Jacob, waiting for him to give up and realize that God is all-powerful and cannot be defeated.

God knows your natural tendency is to fight until you can't fight any more. He would prefer that you and I surrender much earlier but that rarely happens. However, when you choose to surrender to God, only then can He begin to make changes in your life and provide you with the indescribable peace that accompanies intimacy with God.

### 4. Your fight will not stop just because you get tired.

Genesis 32:24 says that *"Jacob was left alone, and a man wrestled with him until daybreak."* Until daybreak! Jacob wrestled all night with God! Why? Because God is not interested in simply ending the fight.

Whining, complaining, and pain will not convince God to stop or give you a break. God will continue to fight, because He is interested in you coming to the point of total dependence on Him. He will continue the fight until the lesson is learned; not just until you come to the point of exhaustion.

Why does God do this, especially when He knows it may hurt you? Because He loves you. He knows that there are things in your life that will never change without a fight. You must struggle with God in order to grow! The Bible repeatedly teaches the principle of brokenness. Brokenness leads to intimacy with God and greater fruitfulness in life. But brokenness does not come without a struggle. And God is willing to continue the fight with you until you break. This is called "tough love."

How long is God willing to fight? As long as it takes. There is an interesting passage in 2 Peter that defines God's long-suffering.

> *"Don't overlook the obvious here, friends. With God, one day is as good as a thousand years, a thousand years as a day. God isn't late with his promise as some measure lateness. He is restraining himself on account of you, holding back the End because He doesn't want anyone lost. He's giving everyone space and time to change."* (2 Peter 3:8-9 MSG)

Your fight may last longer than someone else's fight. God will take as much time as is required. He will fight as long as you resist Him. He will never tire of pursuing you because you were created by Him and for Him.

Do you believe God has given up on you, forgotten you, or let you go? The fight you're in is a reminder that God will NEVER give up on you, nor let you go!

## 5. <u>God will increase the pressure as long as you resist Him.</u>

As long as you continue resisting Him, He will turn up the heat and increase the pressure. Genesis 32:25 says, *"When he saw that he had not prevailed against him, he touched the socket of his thigh; so the socket of Jacob's thigh was dislocated while he wrestled with him."* This is a major injury! This indicates how strongly God will deal with you. As long as you continue to resist God, He will turn up the heat, perhaps even leaving

*Another way God describes this process is as a father would discipline his son. There is pain associated with discipline but the purpose is to restore a broken relationship.*

77

you with permanent scars to show for it. God is trying to get your attention. God dislocated Jacob's hip in order to get his attention. God will do the same with you: increase the pressure so that you turn to Him and become what God has created you to be.

This reminds me of an experience I had in high school as a lifeguard. The first lesson I was taught in my training was that if I saw someone drowning, I was NOT to go in the pool immediately after him. When a person is drowning, he is panicky! The strength of a panicky person who believes they are drowning usually far exceeds the strength of the lifeguard. It is quite likely that if he grabs hold of a lifeguard, they both will go under. A lifeguard is taught to grab something—a towel, pole, ring, or inner tube—to pull the victim to safety with. However, a lifeguard is not to come into direct contact with the victim unless absolutely necessary. In fact, if I had nothing to pull him in with, I was told to wait until the drowning person stops struggling and starts to go under before getting close to the person and dragging the person to safety.

What's the point? God will wait until you finally give up and stop fighting with Him. He will increase the pressure—do whatever is necessary—to get you to submit to Him so that He can draw you close to Him.

Another way God describes this process is as a father would discipline his son. There is pain associated with discipline but the purpose is to restore a broken relationship. The pain is inflicted by the father who loves the son enough to pursue reconciliation. The Bible puts it this way:

> "and you have forgotten the exhortation which is addressed to you as sons, "MY SON, DO NOT REGARD LIGHTLY THE DISCIPLINE OF THE LORD, NOR FAINT WHEN YOU ARE REPROVED BY HIM; 6 FOR THOSE WHOM THE LORD LOVES

*HE DISCIPLINES, AND HE SCOURGES EVERY SON WHOM HE RECEIVES."*
*[7] It is for discipline that you endure; God deals with you as with sons; for what son is there whom his father does not discipline? [8] But if you are without discipline, of which all have become partakers, then you are illegitimate children and not sons. [9] Furthermore, we had earthly fathers to discipline us, and we respected them; shall we not much rather be subject to the Father of spirits, and live? [10] For they disciplined us for a short time as seemed best to them, but He disciplines us for our good, so that we may share His holiness. [11] All discipline for the moment seems not to be joyful, but sorrowful; yet to those who have been trained by it, afterwards it yields the peaceful fruit of righteousness."* (Hebrews 12:5-11 NASB)

God will not avoid fighting with you just because it includes pain. If increasing the pressure will help you become what God intended, He will allow you to suffer! God will allow suffering to bring about change in your life. James 1:2 confirms this: *"Consider it a great joy, my brothers, whenever you experience various trials, knowing that the testing of your faith produces endurance."* God puts the pressure on because He knows that's what it will take for you to submit to His will and become what you were created to be. Though, no doubt about it, it's painful!

**6. God's ultimate objective is that you stop resisting Him and begin to cling to Him.**

Genesis 32:26 says, *"Then he said, 'Let me go, for the dawn is breaking.' But he said, 'I will not let you go unless you bless me.'"* Jacob realized he was losing this battle. He knew it was futile to fight and resist any longer. But, he didn't let go. In fact, he stopped fighting but clung to God. This was the whole point of the fight! God wanted Jacob to stop fighting and resisting Him and start trusting and following Him. The clinging was movement in the right direction. But he still was not ready to start trusting Him. Jacob defaulted back to his negotiation and manipulation mode. He tried to bargain with God and said he would let go when God blessed him. Little did he know that his clinging would lead to the changing of his name and the beginning of an intimate relationship with God.

This concept of "clinging" is what Jesus was referring to when He described the relationship of a *vine* and *branches* in the fifteenth chapter of the Gospel of John. He said the life of the branch was dependent upon its ability to "abide" in the vine. The fruitfulness and productivity of the branch was dependent upon the "abiding" relationship of the vine and the branch. The word "abiding" describes the dependence upon and cooperation of the branch with the vine. Jesus used this illustration to describe one's relationship with God. He said that He was the vine and you were the branch. To "abide" in Jesus meant to live a life so attached to Him that you must rely on Him to live. When His life flows through you, as a branch relies on the vine it is attached to, you would be productive and fruitful.

The purpose of the fight is for you to get to the point where you start abiding in, or clinging to, Christ. *Abide* means to "remain, rest in, and be dependent upon." It is a picture of intimacy. He wants to work in and through your life! God doesn't want you to give up nor does He want to break your spirit; He simply desires to get inside and break your stubborn, self-centered will. Who will ultimately have the right to determine where you go? The abiding factor enables you to be productive in life. This will not happen as long as you continue to resist God and live like an unattached branch. God says He is going to fight until you learn the lesson of clinging versus resisting.

**7. <u>The fight stops when you get honest about your condition.</u>**
Once you get honest about your condition the fighting may stop–temporarily. But that that does not mean the end of the struggle. There will be other fights about other issues in your life. But the fight you are in right now is the one you need to get honest about.

After God and Jacob wrestled until daybreak, Genesis 32:27 says that God asked Jacob his name. God knew who Jacob was but He wanted to see if Jacob finally understood who he really was. Again, the name "Jacob" means "supplanter, manipulator, and the one who gets what he wants." So God asked him, "Who are you?"

Jacob responded by saying his name was "Jacob." In other words he was confessing, "I'm a liar. I'm a manipulator. I'm a supplanter. I'm greedy. That's who I am."

God wants you to be open, honest, and transparent before Him. The fight will stop only when you become honest about who you are. It's at that moment when Proverbs 29:33 and 1 John 1:9 become active in your life:

> *"A person's pride will humble him, but a humble spirit will gain honor,"* and *"On the other hand, if we admit our sins—make a clean breast of them—he won't let us down; he'll be true to himself. He'll forgive our sins and purge us of all wrongdoing."* (MSG)

When I tried out for the wrestling team as a sophomore in high school, I had never before seen an official wrestling match. Some of my friends, who had been on the team, encouraged me to try out, telling me I was guaranteed a spot on the team. I had limited experience and knowledge of the sport, but they reassured me that I would make the team because I was small and there was no one else on the team who would be wrestling in that weight category. I was a proud eighty-nine pounds and just under five-foot tall! I went out for the team and they were right, I made it!

Making the wrestling team was easy. But then I heard that I would have to practice against boys that were heavier than me. The angst I had about that was quickly dissolved when I saw that the guy I would be practicing against was not as strong as I was. He was tall and thin; I was short and compact. The advantage was mine and I was able to win all of our practice sparing matches. This produced within me a false sense of wrestling pride and led me to believe that wrestling someone my weight would be easy.

As a team, we excitedly traveled to our first match. When we arrived and began our warm-ups, I spotted the boy I'd be wrestling with. In my mind I had decided that I had already won; he was scrawny and didn't have a chance! The smallest weight category wrestled first, so as I walked away from the bench onto the mat, I turned toward my team and said: "Boys, watch and learn!"

I was so cocky! I'd never lost—never been given the chance—nor seen anyone else lose. We shook hands, listened to the referee's final instructions, and stepped into position. During the introduction, I thought: "Nobody wants to see a match end so quickly. I'd better play around with him for a little bit and put on a show for the crowd." These thoughts were going through my mind and before I had even decided what I wanted to do, the referee blew the whistle; my opponent picked me up, turned me around, and threw me flat on my back. In the next five seconds, before I was pinned, I thought, "Now what do I do?" The referee slammed his hand on the mat, blew the whistle, and stopped the match. I had lost. We stood up; my opponent's arm was raised in victory, while my head hung in embarrassment and shame.

Now it was time to return to the bench. That was the last thing I wanted to do. My coach shouted: "Landry! Get over here on this bench! Sit down ... and learn!" I was humiliated and embarrassed but pretended like it had never happened. But everyone had seen it! I couldn't believe what had just happened. But, I learned a great lesson that day. It humbled me and motivated me to work harder, pay closer attention, and listen carefully to my coach's instructions. I ended up doing pretty well the rest of the season.

The same lesson must be learned from wrestling matches with God. You must not be proud, thinking you can win. God's objective is for you to abide in Him. Stop resisting Him and start clinging to Him. Be honest and transparent about who you are. When you do that, God can change you, bless you, and transform you into the person He designed you to be!

## 8. Ultimately, every fight with God is a fight over who is in charge.

Every fight you have with God is not about what you have or what you don't have; it's all about who is in charge of your life.

Genesis 32:28 says, *"He said, 'Your name shall no longer be Jacob, but Israel; for you have striven with God and with men and have prevailed.'"* You will not be the same any longer. God knows who you were; you do too. God plans to change your life—change you into a brand new person!

*Every fight you have with God is not about what you have or what you don't have; it's all about who is in charge of your life.*

Jacob now had a new name; a new identity. The name *Israel* literally means, "God rules." In other words, Jacob's life would from this day forward proclaim that God is in charge. God was telling Jacob, "From now on, you will be the one who is known for following the will of God instead of the one that supplants others to get what you want." This would be a radical change!

In the Book of Galatians, the apostle Paul described his radical change this way:

*"I have been crucified with Christ; and it is no longer I who live, but Christ lives in me; and the life which I now live in the flesh I live by faith in the Son of God, who loved me and gave Himself up for me."* (Galatians 2:20 NASB)

Paul expressed his desire to associate with Christ so intimately that he was willing to have his own identity changed. He was renouncing his former right of control over his own life and submitting to a new master, Jesus Christ. This is actually what it means to become a Christian. A Christian is one who has gone to the mat, has surrendered his or her life to Jesus Christ, and is committed to living for Him the rest of his life.

This is a lesson that often requires a lifetime to learn! Know that God will never loosen His grip on you. Be assured that the Scriptures say that once you place your faith in Jesus Christ, you will always be secure in His family! He never lets you go! You may briefly turn your eyes from Jesus and be distracted from His service, but He will never lose focus on you. Unfortunately, this will lead to another fight. The issue, once again is the Lordship of Jesus Christ in your life. Charles Stanley, pastor of the First Baptist Church of Atlanta, Georgia, once preached a message while I was a college student attending his church that has proven helpful to me. The outline is one that I've kept pasted on the inside cover of my Bible to remind me of this vital truth. I share it below to help you as you are evaluating your own life's commitment to Jesus Christ.

**Jesus is Lord of my life ...**
- When I obey the prompting of the Holy Spirit without arguing or fighting back.
- When I am committed to doing His will before I know what it is.
- When I am available to serve Him without regard to the time or place or requirement.

- When pleasing Him takes priority over pleasing all others.
- When I acknowledge and recognize Him as the source of all my desires and needs.
- When I submit to His ownership and possession of all I am and all I have or possess.
- When it is the pattern of my life to turn my failures and defeats and difficulties into opportunities of spiritual growth.
- When to know Him intimately becomes the obsession of my life.

## 9. <u>You will know God won the fight when knowing Him intimately has become the passion of your life.</u>

Isn't it interesting that God asked Jacob his name and then renamed him Israel? Jacob was now to be known as "the one who follows God" or the "one whom God rules over." So what was Jacob's response? Genesis 32:29 says that Jacob then asked God for His name. Jacob was clinging, with everything he had, to this One who had changed his life. Jacob now wanted to know who was responsible for this life changing experience and transformation.

*The blessings of God are always around the corner of intimacy and obedience.*

God didn't respond with His name: *"Then Jacob asked Him and said, 'Please tell me Your name.' But He said, 'Why is it you ask My name?' And He blessed him there." (Genesis 32:29).* Can you imagine the huge smile on God's face during this exchange? Jacob's prayer monologue was now a dialogue that resulted in greater intimacy with God. God's ultimate objective is for you to know Him! Nothing delights God more than when you turn and seek to know Him intimately; which Jacob now wanted.

Do you remember Jacob's previous prayer? He saw God as simply a source of blessing and asked God for that blessing. But now, his desire was simply to know God and to know Him by name. That's when God blessed him. Isn't it interesting? The blessings of God are always around the corner of intimacy and obedience.

Once God has won the wrestling match, you will discover an increasing desire to know Him growing in your heart and mind. The Apostle Paul expressed this in Philippians 3:10-12 (NASB):

> *"That I may know Him and the power of His resurrection and the fellowship of His sufferings, being conformed to His death; [11] in order that I may attain to the resurrection from the dead. [12] Not that I have already obtained it or have already become perfect, but I press on so that I may lay hold of that for which also I was laid hold of by Christ Jesus."*

Paul completely understood the *need* to know God. He was obsessed with knowing Jesus Christ. The reason you are being taken down to the mat with God is because He wants you to know Him! This will not happen until you stop resisting and start clinging to who God is. You will find that He will change who you are, while revealing who He is.

## 10. The scars of your fight with God are intended to be a testimony to others.

Jacob's dislocated hip left him a scar that would be prominent the rest of his life. You will not escape a wrestling match with God without scars. You will be tempted to hide these scars. Don't hide them—show them to others. The scars you bear will give evidence of God and produce hope in the lives of so many who have given up.

Genesis 32:31 explains that Jacob emerged from the fight with scars; he limped because of the pain surrounding his hip. Every limping step would forever remind him of his wrestling match with God. It served as a reminder that he had fought God all night long, but that he had finally stopped resisting God and now devotedly clung to Him. His limp helped him always to be mindful that God had intimately revealed Himself.

Since Jacob's scar was not a hidden one, do you think others noticed the limp? Do you think people asked, "What's wrong with Israel? What happened to him? Didn't that used to be Jacob?" If anyone ever took the time to ask Jacob about his story; his scar became a testimony about what God had done in Jacob's life. His scar revealed to others the patience of God and God's desire to be known and trusted.

You may get nervous or uncomfortable telling others about how God has changed your life. Don't be! There are people who have gone through horrible times, believing God could never love or forgive them. Your scars will remind them of Christ's love and transformation in your own life and give them hope. The scars you bear will open opportunities to talk with people who are wondering whether or not God is real. Your scars may help others see that God is real, active, and alive! Keep talking about your scars and how your life has changed. Never forget what God has done in your life! Psalm 105:5 encourages you in this way: *"Remember His wonders which He has done, His marvels and the judgments uttered by His mouth,"*

> *The scars you bear will give evidence of God and produce hope in the lives of so many who have given up.*

### *How will you respond?*

As a believer, you will never have the influence in your communities or your world until you surrender to God. There will be no "Great Spiritual Awakening" until people like you finally get real with Him. You must stop insisting that you be able to live like you want to live. The Lord Jesus awaits your invitation to sit on the throne of your life. Stop resisting; begin clinging to God and discover who He is and who He created you to be. Slow down at this speed bump.

## QUESTIONS FOR PERSONAL EVALUATION AND DISCUSSION:

1. What are you currently "fighting with God" about?
2. Memorize Galatians 2:20. What does the word "crucify" mean to you? What does it look like for you to 'crucify' yourself?
3. Referring to Dr. Stanley's evaluation list on page 84-85; which 2-3 areas are you struggling to allow Jesus to be LORD?

## PRAYER:

*Heavenly Father, I don't like to fight with You, because You will ultimately always win. Help me, Lord, to humble myself today. Give me the courage to stop resisting you and finally cry "uncle" and let You in! Thank You for this visual of what it means to walk with You and have intimacy with You. It seems kind of strange that it would involve fighting. God, if I am fighting You right now, open my eyes to what is keeping me from resisting You. Help me to turn back to You! Forgive me for always fighting against You and seeking my own way. Help me, Lord, to stop resisting You and start clinging to You. Thank You, God, for the scars I've endured; help me to show those to others and to tell them of how You've changed me and transformed me into a new creation!*

# JACOB

## SPEED BUMPS

- Run away from home after stealing Esau's blessing
- Laban's trickery of giving Rachael instead of Rebecca
- Impending meeting with Esau
- Wrestling match with God

---

## WHAT IS NECESSARY TO CHANGE YOUR PRAYER MONOLOGUE INTO A PRAYER DIALOGUE?

Stop fighting with God and start clinging to Him.

## Chapter 5

# PRAYING FOR A NATION: NEHEMIAH

The United States is often referred to as the "land of the free." This "freedom" is most evident in the ability to exercise our religious beliefs without interference from the government. The First Amendment of the United States Constitution says that the government "shall make no law respecting an establishment of religion, or prohibiting the free exercise thereof..." (United States Constitution, First Amendment).

The first pilgrims to come to America came to gain their religious freedom. This freedom was foundational to the establishment of a new government and thus, it is no surprise that this freedom would be highlighted as the first of ten "Bill of Rights" or "amendments" to the Constitution. Many people gave their lives to gain this freedom. And why would they fight so diligently and passionately? They believed that this freedom was the inherent right of every man and woman created by God.

The founding fathers that penned this important document understood that all freedom originates from God. But that freedom is easily distorted and abused. In fact, one's relationship with God is affected when your freedoms are exaggerated. When the focus of your freedom becomes egocentric rather than God-centered, intimacy with God is not obtainable. This is where the next speed bump comes in. Often God must place a speed bump in your life to slow you down long enough to remind you of the true Source of freedom and the responsibilities associated with that freedom.

A prayer dialogue forces you to move beyond your understanding about freedom and encourages you to listen to God and discover His purpose in giving you freedom. A prayer monologue selfishly leads you to conclude that your freedom has been given so that you can do whatever you want. A prayer dialogue invites God to clarify your understanding of freedom. As you grow in your intimacy with God it becomes apparent that your freedom is provided so that you are better able to accurately represent God in the way you serve and bless others. You'll remember that Jesus said on a number of occasions that He did not come to be served but to serve (Mark 10:45). As Rick Warren has concisely said it in his book, <u>The Purpose Driven Life</u>, "It's not about you."

Unfortunately, when God is conveniently removed from the picture, one's freedom becomes an obsessive pursuit of one's personal desires. It is expressed something like this, "Now that I'm free, I am able to do whatever I want." This kind of attitude concerning freedom actually undermines the very foundation of freedom.

> *A prayer dialogue forces you to move beyond your understanding about freedom and encourages you to listen to God and discover His purpose in giving you freedom.*

I believe the crisis in America today can be attributed to our amnesia about and disrespect for God. It's not about the loss of freedom. We have forgotten both the purpose and Source of freedom. When a nation turns its back on God one can expect an erosion of freedom. Paradoxically, by striving to regain our freedoms we end up losing them. Whenever freedom becomes the ultimate goal, rather than reconciliation and intimacy with God, we are on a collision course for more bondage and less freedom.

You see this repeatedly in the relationship of God and the nation Israel. If you and I are ever to move beyond this massive speed bump, the lessons illustrated by Nehemiah must be learned and applied.

### *The Speed Bump: Praying For A Nation*

In the previous chapters you read about men and women who encountered personal speed bumps along their journey to intimacy with God. In this chapter you will see how God used a man to help a nation maneuver over a terribly destructive speed bump and return to the God who created them to be a blessing to all nations. His name was Nehemiah, and his story shouts loudly concerning the circumstances we similarly face today in America.

In the first chapter of the Book of Nehemiah, we find Nehemiah crying out to the people of God. He calls them to pray to the God they had forsaken. The irony was that Nehemiah was just an ordinary guy. He wasn't a dynamic leader or one of the trained and experienced priests. Rather, Nehemiah was a descendent of the Jewish people who had been conquered and taken prisoner by the Babylonians. He now served as the cupbearer for the king of Persia, who had overthrown the Babylonian Kingdom. While serving in Persia, Nehemiah became concerned about the plight of his people, the Israelites, who had been overthrown and relocated 159 years earlier. Perhaps a brief history lesson here would help.

In 587 B.C., Babylonian King Nebuchadnezzar destroyed the Israelite army and all of Jerusalem. Nebuchadnezzar's men completely leveled the walls of the city and burnt all of the gates. In those days, whenever an army wanted to dishearten a nation and bring it to complete ruin, they tore down their defenses, walls, and gates. This is exactly what Nebuchadnezzar did in Jerusalem. In addition, Nebuchadnezzar took the remaining young and healthy Israelite survivors into captivity and deported them to Babylon. There was no longer an Israelite nation, only survivors. The Jewish homeland had been destroyed, and its people exiled.

Nearly 50 years after the destruction of Jerusalem and 70 years after the first Israelites were taken into captivity, Persia conquered Babylon in 539 B.C. The Persian King Cyrus issued a decree for all exiled Jews to return to their homeland of Jerusalem to rebuild their city and temple. The Israelites rebuilt and dedicated a new temple in 516 B.C. The new temple lacked the size and quality craftsmanship of the enormous and lustrous temple of King Solomon. Although the Jewish nation once again had a temple for worship, it had been built without protective walls or gates.

A second wave of Israelites returned to Jerusalem from captivity in Babylon in approximately 458 B.C. Meanwhile, Nehemiah was serving the current king of Persia, Artaxerxes. Nehemiah heard the reports of the things taking place back in his hometown of Jerusalem and it broke his heart. As the waves of Israelites returned from captivity in Babylon to Israel, they were discouraged at the startling realization that their homeland had been destroyed. The bible describes this in intricate detail in Nehemiah 1:1-11 (NASB).

### *God Is Speaking In The Speed Bump*

Let's pick up the story by reading about Nehemiah's response. You'll notice that his personal pain and brokenness over the circumstances led him to pray. But the prayer reveals a broader understanding of the circumstances. You'll see evidence in his prayer of a response to God rather than simply a cry for a remedy and relief to the current pain. This was the beginning of a prayer dialogue.

> *⁴ When I heard these words, I sat down and wept and mourned for days; and I was fasting and praying before the God of heaven.*
> *⁵ I said, "I beseech You, O LORD God of heaven, the great and awesome God, who preserves the covenant and loving-kindness for those who love*

93

*Him and keep His commandments, ⁶ let Your ear now be attentive and Your eyes open to hear the prayer of Your servant which I am praying before You now, day and night, on behalf of the sons of Israel Your servants, confessing the sins of the sons of Israel which we have sinned against You; I and my father's house have sinned.*

*⁷ "We have acted very corruptly against You and have not kept the commandments, nor the statutes, nor the ordinances which You commanded Your servant Moses.*

*⁸ "Remember the word which You commanded Your servant Moses, saying, 'If you are unfaithful I will scatter you among the peoples; ⁹ but if you return to Me and keep My commandments and do them, though those of you who have been scattered were in the most remote part of the heavens, I will gather them from there and will bring them to the place where I have chosen to cause My name to dwell.'*

*¹⁰ "They are Your servants and Your people whom You redeemed by Your great power and by Your strong hand.*

*¹¹ "O Lord, I beseech You, may Your ear be attentive to the prayer of Your servant and the prayer of Your servants who delight to revere Your name, and make Your servant successful today and grant him compassion before this man." Now I was the cupbearer to the king."* Nehemiah 1:4-11 (NASB)

Nehemiah was truly broken-hearted over the state of his nation. But, Nehemiah was hopeful and appealed to God on His terms for the restoration of the nation of Israel. He firmly believed the words of Psalm 127:1: *"Unless God builds the nation, they that labor, labor in vain."* Nehemiah knew that his only hope was to cry out to the God of Abraham, Isaac, and Jacob.

Nehemiah knew that the people of God had to re-establish a Prayer Dialogue with God. It was time for the people of God to listen to what God had been saying and respond in the way He prescribed. Before there would be any restoration, God would require a national brokenness that would lead to a solemn assembly where the people of God would confess their sin, repent of their former ways, and return to their God. This was a speed bump that could not be ignored.

### *How To Make The Most Of This Speed Bump*

So, what did Nehemiah do? What did he do to call attention to this speed bump? How did this prayer dialogue progress? He started by honestly acknowledging the pitiful and carnal condition of the people of God.

### 1. Be alert to the spiritual condition of God's people.

The first lesson that Nehemiah teaches is to honestly look at the spiritual condition of the yourself and the people of God and keep it in mind as you maneuver over the speed bump. In other words, recognize that the current attitudes and lifestyles of God's people will impact their ability to deal with this speed bump. We must resist the temptation to close our eyes and pretend

*Are you overly concerned about today at the expense of tomorrow?*

nothing is wrong. Hiding and hoping that everything will fix itself is not a plausible solution. We must stay alert the way Nehemiah did; he realistically understood what the people of Israel were experiencing. He knew how they were living and what they believed. He started there.

Now read Nehemiah 1:3:

95

*"The remnant there in the province who survived the captivity are in great distress and reproach, and the wall of Jerusalem is broken down and its gates are burned with fire."*

- **People are in a survival mode.**
  Nehemiah noticed that Jews were struggling to live daily. They were not thinking about the future, much less rebuilding a nation or becoming themselves a "great" people once more. The Jews were merely trying to *"survive."* Does that sound familiar? Have you forgotten why God blesses a nation? Are you overly concerned about today at the expense of tomorrow? Has your routine of life so consumed your thinking and time that intimacy with God is no longer a hope to be pursued?

- **People are in distress.**
  The Jews didn't know what to do or even if they were going to make it. They were in *"great distress."* They felt powerless; they were so concerned about their daily problems that they just gave up on any future changes. Again, does that sound like today? Foreclosures, financial failures, inflation, increasing fuel prices, the uncertainty of the future; these are all signs of people in distress.

- **People are living dishonorably.**
  The Israelites had adopted a lifestyle of compromise and *"reproach."* Their way of life was disgraceful in the eyes of God. In order to survive, they felt they had to compromise the truth. As a nation of people, they gave up things that were very sacred to them, such as abiding by the Law of Moses concerning marriage. Jews began to marry non-Jews; which was clearly forbidden in the Old Testament law. When people redefine marriage as something different from what God intended and has

96

prescribed, they are guilty of compromising the truth. Does this sound familiar?

We are as guilty today as the Israelites were then. Nationally our solutions concerning marriage have become ones that compromise God's standards and are just as dishonorable before God. As you approach God to engage in a *Prayer Dialogue* about the nation, we must be honest about where we are, individually, as well as part of a whole. The moral erosion of our nation has occurred to a large degree because God's people have identified with a pragmatic, yet godless, proverb, "*The ends justify the means.*"

*As you approach God to engage in a Prayer Dialogue about the nation, we must be honest about where we are, individually, as well as part of a whole.*

For example, a recent interview with graduating high school students, revealed that they were willing to do whatever it took, including stealing or cheating on tests, to get into the college of their choice. Their rationale was that "the ends justify the means." They clung to a faulty circular argument. It sounded like this: "There's nothing wrong with cheating because it's more important that I get into college. If I don't get into college then I won't be able to do what I really want to do. So I've got to do what it takes to get into college, even if that means cheating. Cheating can't be wrong because it's getting me where I need to go." Notice the self-centeredness of this argument. Again, when freedom becomes the obsession of simply getting what one wants, it ceases to be the freedom that was originally designed by God and intended to be enjoyed by all.

- **People are defenseless.** Nehemiah 1:3 talks about the walls and gates of Jerusalem being destroyed. When Jerusalem had walls and gates, they were able to defend themselves. Without this protection, they knew it would be only a matter of time before someone else would enslave them.

America is in the same defenseless situation with a different kind of wall. Its "walls" are being torn down daily in our court system. Laws are being revoked that were originally established to protect our freedom. Some may believe the solution is simply in appointing conservative Supreme Court Justices that will uphold traditional understandings of Constitutional law. However, we must never forget that the Supreme Court is not responsible for the morality, or immorality of America.

> *However, we must never forget that the Supreme Court is not responsible for the morality, or immorality of America.*

The original lawmakers established moral laws and attempted to personally live moral lives because they believed in God and that He was Himself moral by nature. They felt responsible to the one, true God who establishes those moral boundaries. What America really needs now is a change of heart among the people of God within her borders, not just her leaders.

America's Founding Fathers knew that there could not be any laws or legislation based on morality without first acknowledging the existence of a moral God. George Washington, a Founding Father and first President of our nation, referred to this in his farewell speech as President on September 19, 1796.

*"It is impossible to govern the world without God and the Bible... Of all the dispositions and habits that lead to political prosperity, our religion and morality are the indispensable supporters... let us with caution indulge the supposition that morality can be maintained without religion... reason and experience both forbid us to expect that our national morality can prevail in exclusion of religious principle."* [Original Intent by David Barton, p. 117]

Washington knew exactly why America would stand strong: God's providence and blessing. Even Ben Franklin, who is not known for his Christian commitment, said that American success and freedom cannot be separated from God.

*"I have lived, sir, a long time, and the longer I live, the more convincing proofs I see of this truth—that God governs in the affairs of men. And if a sparrow cannot fall to the ground without His notice, is it probable that an empire can rise without His aid? We have been assured, sir, in the Sacred Writings, that 'except the Lord build the House, they labor in vain that build it.' I firmly believe this, and I also believe that without His concurring aid we shall succeed in this political building no better than the builders of Babel; we shall be divided by our little partial local interests; our projects will be confounded, and we ourselves shall become a reproach and*

*When people try to take God out of the freedom equation in an attempt not to infringe on other people's rights, the country becomes defenseless.*

*byword down to future ages." [Original Intent by David Barton, p. 111)*

John Adams, the second President of the United States, in an address to military leaders said this:

*"We have no government armed with the power capable of contending with human passions, unbridled by morality and true religion. Our Constitution was made only for a moral and religious people. It is wholly inadequate to the government of any other." [Original Intent by David Barton, p. 182]*

When people try to take God out of the freedom equation in an attempt not to infringe on other people's rights, the country becomes defenseless. Walls are torn down, and gates are destroyed. The only real solution begins with the humble acknowledgement of the spiritual condition of the people of God. Alertness to this condition and honest confession of one's personal guilt is the beginning of the restoration of a prayer dialogue. Pray not just for certain appointments of God-fearing people to be elected to government positions; but also specifically pray for a heart change in the people of God, like yourself, who live in America.

## 2. Personally identify with the nation.
The second lesson Nehemiah teaches is to personally identify with the nation. He did not merely sit back and blame others, even though the destruction of his homeland was the result of the rebellion of a people of God from an entirely different generation. He identified with the pain of the people. Nehemiah 1:4 says, *"When I heard these words, I sat down and wept and mourned for days; and I was fasting and praying before the God of heaven."*

- **Let it bother you.** Nehemiah let the situation bother him, and you need to let what is happening in America bother you, as well. When was the last time you were deeply saddened over the spiritual and moral condition of your nation? It is time to truly and deeply care for your nation! The current condition of our nation must grieve you personally before you can honestly expect God to restore our country. Engage your heart and mind—it's going to break your heart.

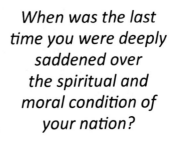

*When was the last time you were deeply saddened over the spiritual and moral condition of your nation?*

- **Be patient.** Nehemiah admitted that he *"mourned for a number of days."* He knew it was going to take a long time to truly turn around his country, but he was willing to wait. He knew that he needed to come to God on His terms, rather than demand God meet him on his terms.

### 3. Pray specifically.

The third lesson Nehemiah teaches is to be specific as you pray. He knew it was now time to plead with God for help. It was time to approach God on His terms with prayer. This prayer dialogue could not be a generic prayer to some generic god. It would need to be a specific prayer to a God who has already revealed Himself to His people. That is why he first appealed to God on the basis of His covenant.

- **Approach God on the basis of His covenant.** The only way you will successfully connect with God is when you approach Him on His terms—through His covenant. You cannot expect God to help simply because you are in need. You can, however, be confident that God will respond on the basis of your covenantal relationship with Him. Notice how Nehemiah phrased his prayer:

*"I said, "I beseech You, O LORD God of heaven, the great and awesome God, who preserves the covenant and lovingkindness for those who love Him and keep His commandments."* (Nehemiah 1:5).

Nehemiah simply reminded God of the covenantal terms of Israel's relationship with Him. He was referring to an incident that was recorded in Genesis 12, when God committed Himself to Abraham. He told Abraham that He would bless him and make him a blessing to all nations. Later, God revealed to His people that He would bless them as long as they loved Him and kept His commands. Their disobedience would result in curses rather than blessings. That is ultimately what happened.

Nehemiah came to God on God's terms, telling Him that he knew the blessing of God would not return apart from the loyal obedience of His people. This was the basis of the covenant.

There are two lessons to learn from this. First, God can be always be trusted to honor His commitments to you. Second, you are unable to honor your part of the agreement. There is no way that anyone can completely keep all the commands of God. The

*God's speed bump brought them to a point where they would dependently cry out to Him. Once they abandoned the pride and arrogance of self-centeredness and personal agendas, God was able to empower them with His grace to rediscover the intimate relationship they had once before enjoyed with God.*

Israelites demonstrated this time and time again. However, this failure of God's people to keep His law alienated them from the God who created and loved them. Eventually it would lead to a brokenness of heart that resulted in a humble cry to the same God for forgiveness and a restoration of the intimate and covenantal relationship they had once experienced.

God's speed bump brought them to a point where they would dependently cry out to Him. Once they abandoned the pride and arrogance of self-centeredness and personal agendas, God was able to empower them with His grace to rediscover the intimate relationship they had once before enjoyed with God. This same motif was expressed through the prophet Jeremiah when He described the new covenant that He intended to establish.

> *"But this is the covenant which I will make with the house of Israel after those days," declares the LORD, "I will put My law within them and on their heart I will write it; and I will be their God, and they shall be My people.*
> *[34] "They will not teach again, each man his neighbor and each man his brother, saying, 'Know the LORD,' for they will all know Me, from the least of them to the greatest of them," declares the LORD, "for I will forgive their iniquity, and their sin I will remember no more."* (Jeremiah 31:33-34 NASB)

God declares that it's not about how well you can keep His commandments; it's about your desire and commitment to know Him personally and intimately. Forgiveness and cleansing of guilt is only possible in the context of this kind of relationship. The new covenant is based on the old covenant, which reveals that God is faithful and initiates the relationship. It also identifies a major problem—man is unable to reciprocate in this relationship by perfectly keeping His law.

That's why He sent Jesus! Jesus came and died on the cross to take care of your sin problem. We are all born sinners, and that sin separates you from God. He sent Jesus to pay the penalty of your sin; that penalty is death. He was willing to personally pay for your sin. The price for your sin had to be paid for reconciliation to be a reality. So Jesus was sent to earth to die in your place and be resurrected on the third day in order that you may receive as a gift His amazing eternal life.

All you have to do is, by faith, open the door and invite Him into your life. At that moment, you'll be forgiven. Then you have the right to approach God. You can know what God is all about and respond to His promptings and live according to His plan for your life.

### 4. Pray with a submissive attitude.
Nehemiah prayed:

> "Let Your ear now be attentive and Your eyes open to hear the prayer of Your servant which I am praying before You now, day and night, on behalf of the sons of Israel Your servants, confessing the sins of the sons of Israel which we have sinned against You; I and my father's house have sinned." (Nehemiah 1:6 NASB)

Nehemiah did not come to God to tell Him what to do. He said: "God, I'm coming to serve You because You are God. I'm coming to You on Your terms. I'm here at Your disposal. I'm coming to You on behalf of sinful people and as Your servant. What would You have us to do?"

That's how to pray for America! Pray specifically and come to God on His terms. You must have that relationship or covenant with Him. You come to Him, not to tell Him what needs to happen or what He needs to do (e.g. who needs to be in the White House or on the Supreme Court). You can pray about those things, but don't let it be your main agenda. Your agenda should be to say, "God, I'm here to serve You. How can I serve You?" Then you can expect God to remove the speed bump and allow you to move forward.

- **<u>Confess sin—personal and national.</u>** God wants you to confess your personal sins, as well as the sins of the nation. Americans must stop shifting the blame and complaining that we aren't responsible for the problems in our country. We have to be willing to say, "God, I blew it and so did my country. I am responsible, too."

  The word *confession* is not a complicated word to understand. It comes from the Greek word *homologeo* (*homou* means "the same" and *lego* means "to say"). So when you confess your sin, you are simply saying the same thing God has been saying all along. For example, when God says, "You blew it," He's expecting you to admit it. Instead, you may say, "Well, there's a reason I blew it. I wouldn't have blown it if so-and-so wasn't in my life or if You had done such-and-such for me." See the difference? You've transferred the guilt. You are no longer confessing sin but making excuses for it.

  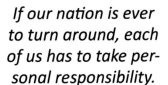

  *If our nation is ever to turn around, each of us has to take personal responsibility.*

  If our nation is ever to turn around, each of us has to take personal responsibility. Nehemiah understood this and accordingly prayed in this way:

*"We have acted very corruptly against You and have not kept the commandments, nor the statutes, nor the ordinances which You commanded Your servant Moses.[8] "Remember the word which You commanded Your servant Moses, saying, 'If you are unfaithful I will scatter you among the peoples."* (Nehemiah 1:6-7 NASB)

Like Nehemiah, we need to pray for our land and be willing to confess our sins before God.

- **<u>Expect God to follow through with His promises</u>**. Nehemiah reminded God about His promise to the Israelite nation in verse 8-9:

*"Remember the word which You commanded Your servant Moses, saying, 'If you are unfaithful I will scatter you among the peoples;[9] but if you return to Me and keep My commandments and do them, though those of you who have been scattered were in the most remote part of the heavens, I will gather them from there and will bring them to the place where I have chosen to cause My name to dwell.'"*

God promised two things to the Israelites: If they messed up then they would be completely scattered; however, if they came back, they'd be gathered together and be a blessing once again.

There are a lot of people who presume God wants to restore America. I want to believe that, too; but what if strengthening America isn't in God's ultimate plan for mankind? Are you okay with that? What if this country is going to fail? You must come to God on the basis of His promises, fully trusting His omnipotent leadership for our world, not merely what you hope His plan is. So look for the promises of God. He gives us a great promise in 2 Chronicles 7:14:

*"And if My people who are called by My name humble themselves, pray and seek My face, and turn from their evil ways, then I will hear from heaven, forgive their sin, and heal their land."*

What's the promise? *"I will forgive their sin, and heal their land."* If you're going to pray specifically for your nation, then expect God to follow through on His promises. However, there are conditions to these promises that we need to fulfill. Notice that it doesn't say that if the entire nation will humble itself. It says, "If my people (that's you and me)." In other words, "If the people, who claim to be followers of Jesus Christ, will humble themselves and pray, then God will hear. If they turn from their wicked ways, then He'll hear and forgive their sins."

- **Ask God to empower you to be part of the solution.** When you humble yourself and live as God's servant and begin praying with a submissive attitude, do not be surprised when God calls you to be a part of the solution. You may oftentimes want to put the "reward" part first. If you get busy, you can fit God in another time when you are less busy. However, Nehemiah says,

*"O Lord, I beseech You, may Your ear be attentive to the prayer of Your servant and the prayer of Your servants who delight to revere Your name, and make Your servant successful today and grant him compassion before this man." Now I was the cupbearer to the king."* (Nehemiah 1:11)

After Nehemiah had prayed everything before verse 11, he said he was willing to be available. In other words, he believed God had placed him in his role as the cupbearer to the king, and he was asking God to help him leverage his position and influence with the king. He asked God to give him boldness and wisdom to tell the king what God wanted him to.

### *How will you respond?*

All of us need to pray. If our nation is to survive and continue to be a blessing and positive influence on other nations, then we need to enter into a prayer dialogue with God. This dialogue must begin by humbly acknowledging the source of our freedom. This speed bump is intended to slow us down long enough to remember the responsibility associated with this freedom. Our influence on others will always be shaped by the way we exercise or abuse our freedoms.

*If our nation is to survive and continue to be a blessing and positive influence on other nations, then we need to enter into a prayer dialogue with God.*

Disregarding this speed bump will not only eventually rob us of our current freedoms but also prevent us from being a positive influence on others. We can expect the journey that ignores this speed bump to result in a moral collapse from within while creating confusion, dishonor, and disgrace. The future of a free America will ultimately depend on the response of the people of God to the speed bumps He has placed before them. In other words, the future of this country, as it did with Israel in Nehemiah's time, depends on our *Prayer Dialogues* with God. No longer ignorant, we know what we have to do. It's time to pray.

## QUESTIONS FOR PERSONAL EVALUATION AND DISCUSSION:

1. Discuss the difference between "freedom in Christ" vs. "freedom without Christ." What is the ultimate purpose of God giving 'freedom?'
2. Summarize Nehemiah 1:1-11. What was Nehemiah broken over and what did he do about it?
3. Stop and evaluate the context and culture of our day. What are the immediate issues, outside of your personal life, that needs prayer? Take some time on your knees in prayer dialoguing with God about these issues.

## PRAYER:

*Father, I thank You for the example and Prayer Dialogue of Nehemiah. I confess on behalf of all of us that we are a selfish, self-centered people. We have been so blessed that we are becoming more concerned about preserving our blessings than becoming a blessing to others. Lord, we are guilty of blaming everybody else for our problems, when we've not been the light or the salt that we've needed. Please forgive us. We've come to you on our terms and told you what you've needed to do, rather than come to you on our terms and offered ourselves as servants. Please forgive us. Lord, forgive my personal sins, as well as the nation's sins. Use me to be part of the solution. I am humbling myself today, praying with submission to Your will, dear Lord. Please heal our land.*

# NEHEMIAH

## SPEED BUMPS

- Heart broken over the condition of Jerusalem and discouraged Israelites
- Speak honestly with King Artexerses
- Prayer as a beginning point

---

## WHAT IS NECESSARY TO CHANGE YOUR PRAYER MONOLOGUE INTO A PRAYER DIALOGUE?

See freedom as liberty and opportunity to serve others.

## Chapter 6

# MOVING OUTSIDE YOUR COMFORT ZONE: ANANIAS

W hile looking for a good illustration about how people respond to change I came across a humorous excerpt in my files from a supposed local New England newspaper during a time when gas streetlights were first being proposed to its community. This supposedly *fictional* article couldn't be any clearer about how people exaggerate and rationalize their case when looking for reasons not to change.

The local paper published four primary objections:

1. A Spiritual Objection – "Artificial illumination would interfere with the divine plan, because the world is supposed to be dark in the night hours."
2. A Medical Objection – "Emanations from illuminating gas would be dangerous, and therefore these lighted streets would incline people to stay indoors which would then increase the number of people with colds."
3. A Moral Objection – "The fear of darkness would vanish, and drunkenness and depravity would most assuredly increase."
4. A Popular Objection – "If the streets were illuminated every night, such constant illumination would tend to rob festive occasions of their charm."

The objections are hilarious. Of course, that's easy to say after the fact. But when faced with the reality of impending change and the threat of moving outside your comfort zone, it's so easy to manufacture objections that seem reasonable at the time. Isn't it amazing how quickly you can rationalize away innovation that may improve your life because of the potential threat it may be to your currently satisfying situation? The fear of the unknown can be debilitating and confusing. Irrationality quickly takes the place of clear thinking when faced with changes you cannot understand. If not careful, you'll find yourself defaulting to your "comfort zone" setting and completely miss a change that would prove beneficial to you. This natural tendency to avoid change and remain within our comfort zone is a speed bump worth investigating further.

### The Speed Bump: Moving Outside Your Comfort Zone

Ananias struggled with this speed bump. We find his story in the book of Acts, chapter 9. We first find him praying, engaged in a lively *Prayer Dialogue* with God. God then tells him to do something that he really didn't want to do. His hesitancy to obey God became a speed bump that helped to more clearly define his current relationship with God. Ananias suggested that God find someone else. The assignment, in his opinion, was too risky and he didn't want to go down that road.

Before we go any further, it's important that we look at another biblical snapshot of a character named Saul. He would ultimately become better know as the apostle Paul, but at this time his name had yet to be changed; it was still Saul of Tarsus. He was devoutly Jewish, a Pharisee, and aspired to become a strong leader in the religious ruling body named the Sanhedrin.

Saul was rabid in his opposition to Christianity. He viewed Christians as blasphemers of his faith and he sought to eradicate them. In fact, he was present, and gave his consent when one of the Christian disciples named Stephen was stoned to death. After the stoning, Saul requested and obtained authorization from the Sanhedrin to go to Damascus and arrest everyone who claimed to be a follower of Jesus and bring them back to Jerusalem for trial. Let's look at Acts 9:3-9 and see what happened next.

> *³ As he was traveling, it happened that he was approaching Damascus, and suddenly a light from heaven flashed around him; ⁴ and he fell to the ground and heard a voice saying to him, "Saul, Saul, why are you persecuting Me?" ⁵ And he said, "Who are You, Lord?" And He said, "I am Jesus whom you are persecuting, ⁶ but get up and enter the city, and it will be told you what you must do."*
> *⁷ The men who traveled with him stood speechless, hearing the voice but seeing no one.*
> *⁸ Saul got up from the ground, and though his eyes were open, he could see nothing; and leading him by the hand, they brought him into Damascus. ⁹ And he was three days without sight, and neither ate nor drank."*

## God Is Speaking In The Speed Bump

This passage provides the setting for Ananias' struggle. Saul went to Damascus with orders to arrest any and all Christians. While traveling, he was struck by God and blinded. His companions had to personally assist him as he made it the rest of the way to Damascus. In this blinding confrontation, God spoke to Saul about what to expect once he arrived in the city. He was to meet a follower of Jesus named Ananias.

Now, try to put yourself in Ananias' shoes as you continue to read what happened next:

> *"Now there was a disciple at Damascus named Ananias; and the Lord said to him in a vision, "Ananias." And he said, "Here I am, Lord." ¹¹ And the Lord said to him, "Get up and go to the*

*street called Straight, and inquire at the house of Judas for a man from Tarsus named Saul, for he is praying, $^{12}$ and he has seen in a vision a man named Ananias come in and lay his hands on him, so that he might regain his sight."*
*$^{13}$ But Ananias answered, "Lord, I have heard from many about this man, how much harm he did to Your saints at Jerusalem; $^{14}$ and here he has authority from the chief priests to bind all who call on Your name.' "* (Acts 9:10-14 NASB)

Imagine what Ananias must have thought when he heard these words from God. I envision him saying something like this: "God, please don't make me do this. This is too much to ask, and I really don't want to do it. I've got kids and a family to worry about. Saul could arrest me and imprison me...maybe even kill me! Please don't make me do this!"

But notice what God said in response and watch what Ananias did:

*"$^{15}$ But the Lord said to him, "Go, for he is a chosen instrument of Mine, to bear My name before the Gentiles and kings and the sons of Israel; $^{16}$ for I will show him how much he must suffer for My name's sake."*
*$^{17}$ So Ananias departed and entered the house, and after laying his hands on him said, "Brother Saul, the Lord Jesus, who appeared to you on the road by which you were coming, has sent me so that you may regain your sight and be filled with the Holy Spirit."*
*$^{18}$ And immediately there fell from his eyes something like scales, and he regained his sight, and he got up and was baptized; $^{19}$ and he took food and was strengthened. Now for several days he*

114

*was with the disciples who were at Damascus, [20] and immediately he began to proclaim Jesus in the synagogues, saying, "He is the Son of God." [21] All those hearing him continued to be amazed, and were saying, "Is this not he who in Jerusalem destroyed those who called on this name, and who had come here for the purpose of bringing them bound before the chief priests?"' "* (Acts 9:15-21 NASB)

What an amazing story! Ananias had an encounter with God that significantly enhanced his intimacy with God. Though his reluctance to obey God functioned as a temporary speed bump in the relationship, he finally did move beyond the security of his comfort zone and chose to do what God was asking of him.

God spoke directly to him, as you would expect in a *Prayer Dialogue*. Now it was up to Ananias to respond. To resist God's will was to settle for a *Prayer Monologue*. This would definitely be a step in the wrong direction.

I want to clarify something here. Prayer Dialogues require honesty. It's all right to express your fears and reservations concerning God's plans for you. The move from a *Prayer Dialogue* to a *Prayer Monologue* occurs the moment you reject God's message and begin treating Him as someone who exists to serve you. Ananias could think of many reasons why he was not the right man for this job, but he was

> *The move from a Prayer Dialogue to a Prayer Monologue occurs the moment you reject God's message and begin treating Him as someone who exists to serve you.*

honest enough to talk to God about them. He also ultimately obeyed God.

115

Observing Ananias' *Prayer Dialogue* with God, you can see that it involved being honest with God. However, just because you are honest does not mean that you are going to get what you want or change God's mind. When God speaks to you, He always has His ultimate plan in mind. You can expect Him to constantly remind you what He created you for, what He created you to do, and what He created you to become. Just because you know, however, doesn't mean you'll be very eager to experience it.

### How To Make The Most Of This Speed Bump

So how are you supposed to make it over this kind of speed bump and not miss God's best? How did Ananias maneuver over this speed bump? Let's look a little closer at the story.

### 1. Do not skip the starting point.

If you truly desire to make it over this speed bump, you must begin with an honest assessment of your relationship with God. You have to start right in order to finish right. There is a word that describes the starting point of Ananias—*disciple.* *"Now there was a disciple at Damascus named Ananias. And the Lord said to him in a vision, 'Ananias!' And he said, 'Here I am, Lord!'" Acts 9:10 (NASB)*

What is a disciple? From the earliest days of the church the word disciple has been a synonym for Christian. In other words, this means that Ananias had sometime earlier been confronted with the claims and life of Jesus Christ and placed his faith in Him. Ananias was not perfect but he was *born again.*

This is a prerequisite to any *Prayer Dialogue.* There must be a spiritual connection between you and God before a *Prayer Dialogue* can begin. The Apostle Paul describes this connection in his letter to the church at Ephesus,

> *"In Him, you also, after listening to the message*
> *of truth, the gospel of your salvation-having also*

116

*believed, you were sealed in Him with the Holy Spirit of promise, who is given as a pledge of our inheritance, with a view to the redemption of God's own possession, to the praise of His glory."* (Eph 1:13-14 NASB)

This starting point is so important. Just because you may have been raised in a Christian home or regularly attended church as you were growing up doesn't mean you are a *disciple*. The truth is that you, and everyone else, are born disconnected from Jesus Christ. You don't gradually become a disciple simply by spending time with other professing disciples. There comes a time in each person's life when they must make a personal decision to follow Jesus and receive His gift of eternal life. You can expect God to convict you of this need for forgiveness and a new life. Once acknowledged and received by faith, your repentant response transforms you into a "disciple."

God has provided everything necessary for you to make that kind of decision. However, He will never make the decision for you. God desires to connect with you, but He will never force that choice upon you. You have been created with the ability to make your own choices. You have been given a free will.

God loved mankind so much that He sent His Son, Jesus, to die on a cross to pay your sin debt. This death removed the obstacle to reconciliation and thus gives you and me the gracious and merciful option of turning to Him. Three days later, Jesus rose from the grave—alive! Because of that, He now offers you eternal life. This is the beginning of a personal connection and intimate relationship with Him. All that remains for you to do is simply receive this gracious gift from God.

There is not another way connect to God. Everyone has to approach Him this way. If you are going to be connected with Jesus Christ, if you're going to be a disciple, you must start right.

However, a disciple is someone who is more than just connected. A disciple is someone who, soon after placing his faith in Jesus, identifies himself with the name of Jesus through baptism. Baptism is a disciple's way to publicly profess faith in Christ. The picture is perfect. Going under the water is a picture of the death and burial of Jesus while coming back out of the water is picture of the resurrection of Jesus. When you are baptized you are preaching the gospel without saying a word.

This is the where it begins. This is the starting point that cannot be skipped. You don't have to be in a church service for this to happen either. If you feel like you cannot wait any longer, whisper a prayer to God right now. Say, "God, before I read anything else, I want to be connected to You. I believe Jesus Christ died for me, and I humbly accept the gift of eternal life that you offer. I choose to repent of my sins and trust You only for this new life.

That's the starting point. Don't skip it! Perhaps the purpose of this speed bump was to slow you down long enough to start right.

## 2. Spiritual growth requires an intentional focus on God.

God's plan includes spiritual growth. But you will only grow as you're paying attention to God. This is especially difficult when your painful circumstances scream for relief.

But you are on the cusp of spiritual growth when God has exposed your insistence to remain in your comfort zone.

You can see this as God confronts Ananias. *"Now there was a disciple at Damascus named Ananias. And the Lord said to him in a vision, 'Ananias!' And he said, 'Here I am, Lord!'"* (Acts 9:10) In this case, God chose to use a vision to speak to Ananias. But notice his response, "Here I am, Lord!" He was paying attention. He was deliberately listening for a word from God. If you are paying attention to God, you will see that He uses many ways to speak to you. Sometimes God speaks in a vision and at other times a dream. At other times, God will speak to you through a trusted counselor or friend. God can even use your painful circumstances to get your attention. But I believe that most often, God will speak to you through the Bible.

*But you are on the cusp of spiritual growth when God has exposed your insistence to remain in your comfort zone.*

Have you ever read a part of the Scripture and felt like it was a personal message to you? It was at that time when God was speaking to you. But, if you're not paying attention when He speaks, the words will seem to be merely organized ink marks on a page.

While God will use whatever it takes to get through to you, know that the problem is not with the scarcity of His speech. He is always speaking to us. The problem is not whether God is speaking; the problem is that you and I are not paying attention or listening when He does speak.

It is necessary to train yourself to hear God by setting aside time to listen to Him. This kind of focus requires discipline and determination. Daily decisions to get quiet and alone with God will fine-tune your listening ability. But silence alone is not enough. When you choose to be silent, that is the perfect time to saturate your mind and heart with the Scriptures.

I recommend that you establish, if you've not already, a daily habit of reading the Bible. As you are reading, expect to hear from God. Honestly, He wants to speak to you more than you want to hear from Him. Look for Him to reveal His heart and expose your heart and mind to the truth as you read His Word. But don't be surprised when God speaks in an unexpected manner. Your desire for Him to communicate in a predictable way may actually cause you to miss Him when He does speak.

Sometimes the silence can seem unbearable when you're anxious to hear from God. And often, when you're anticipating a certain response from God the silence may be the result of refusing to hear the truth. But God is waiting for you to get still long enough to listen to Him, because He wants to speak to you; He wants to transform your life.

When God spoke in a vision to Ananias, he was paying attention and responded, "Here I am, Lord!" Are you paying enough attention to be able to respond, "Here I am, Lord" when God speaks? That is why your personal devotion time is often called a "quiet time." It is a time for you to stop everything, become still, and tell God you are ready to listen to what He wants to say. The more disciplined you become with these quiet moments of listening, the more often you will hear God when He speaks.

Listen to the following verse from the Psalmist. It often convicts me during my times of busyness when I am tempted to drive over the speed bumps in my life without slowing down.

> *"O God, You are my God; I shall seek You earnestly; My soul thirsts for You, my flesh yearns for You, In a dry and weary land where there is no water."* (Psalm 63:1 NASB)

Is that how you seek God? Are you desperate to hear from Him? Does your soul feel thirsty, dry, or desolate? Do you allow this dryness and desperation motivate you to seek God every day. Go on...go to God right now and confess your eagerness to hear from Him; tell Him that you must have a word from Him and have His involvement in your life. When you come to God

*It is necessary to train yourself to hear God by setting aside time to listen to Him.*

that way, every day, attentively, you will hear from God.

### 3. God's plan for you concerns others.

God is very specific in His plan for Ananias:

*"And the Lord said to him, 'Get up and go to the street called Straight, and inquire at the house of Judas for a man from Tarsus named Saul, for he is praying,'"* (Acts 9:11 NASB)

From previous verses, you know the record of Saul. So you can understand why Ananias was reluctant to follow God's instructions. However, God's plan for Ananias involved impacting another person's life that would ultimately impact the world.

Once you have connected with Christ, you will see that His plan for your life is about influencing others. And most often, this influence begins with a willingness to serve others. God's mission for you is the same as it was for Jesus: *"Just as the Son of Man did not come to be served, but to serve, and to give His life a ransom for many"* (Matthew 20:28 NASB)

> *Once you have connected with Christ, you will see that His plan for your life is about influencing others.*

Did you know that God is putting people in your life right now who are wishing that someone would come to them with answers about how they can connect with God? In my experience, there is currently a great spiritual sensitivity among all age groups. People can't help but sense an inner emptiness that appears to be "God-shaped." They aren't exactly sure how to describe this emptiness but they know there is something missing. They've been seeking answers from the entertainment world, religious leaders, educators, the financially successful, medical professionals and the government. Having yet to get real answers to their questions, they are still on the search for somebody, somebody like you, who will point them to the God who created them for Himself and with a fulfilling purpose.

You, as a follower of Jesus Christ, already know the answer. There is only one answer, *"Jesus told him, 'I am the way, the truth, and the life. No one comes to the Father except through Me' "* (John 14:6 NASB)

If God has changed your life, tell people about it! There is nothing condescending or judgmental about it. Tell others about what God has done in your life. If others don't want to listen, that is their prerogative. But you must be on the alert for the people God puts in your path. You must keep in mind that they are desperately searching for answers and solutions and often don't even know what questions to ask.

*They aren't exactly sure how to describe this emptiness but they know there is something missing.*

Sharing your faith will move you outside of your comfort zone. American Christians are often discouraged from talking to others about faith issues because they say it requires imposing beliefs on someone else. This couldn't be further from the truth. There is no imposing of anything. Sharing your faith with another person should stimulate their thinking. It should cause them to question their own beliefs and re-examine whether they stand the test of truth and reality. The other person is free to believe or not believe what you are sharing.

If you had discovered the cure for cancer, you would not be fearful of imposing your knowledge about that cure on a person who has cancer. You wouldn't be concerned that they might think you are being too pushy, too confident in what you've discovered, or too excited about the potential cure. You would compel them to apply the cure! You would tell them again and again, pleading with them to listen!

God's plan will always involve your influencing others. Move beyond this speed bump of fear and reluctance by initiating conversations about Jesus. Today, take some time to share with another person the incredible change and connection you have experienced in Jesus and how they can experience it also.

## 4. Expect God to prepare others for your obedience.

God instructed Ananias to talk to Saul. Ananias did not personally know Saul but had heard about his reputation. But God empowered Ananias to get over this speed bump by informing him that He had prepared Saul for their meeting. Knowing that God prepares both people in a divinely planned encounter is intended to have the same effect on you.

God is not just going to say "go talk to so-and-so" without preparing that person ahead of time. God is, at this very moment, preparing people to whom you will talk. You may not know who that person is right now, but it doesn't hurt to ask. This is at the heart of a *Prayer Dialogue*. Ask God—then listen for a response. Pause right now and ask God to prompt you, to put a name or a face on your mind. Write his or her name down in the margin of this book. Perhaps the phone will ring and it will be that one whom God has been preparing. You never know how God will answer when you choose to listen.

Acts 9:12 says: *"and he has seen in a vision a man named Ananias come in and lay his hands on him, so that he might regain his sight."* Here we have God telling Ananias to go talk to Saul and that Saul would be expecting him. What do you suppose went through Ananias' mind? I'm sure he still felt uncomfortable. He probably still wanted out of this arrangement.

> *This is at the heart of a Prayer Dialogue. Ask God – then listen for a response.*

He probably still hoped that God would change His mind.

Is that what you would say to God if you had been Ananias? We can always invent excuses. But God has a plan, and His plan is for you to talk with others about Him. To accomplish that, He will always uniquely prepare that person for you.

When I lived in Ohio, I had the opportunity to speak at the revival services of a church in a neighboring town. The pastor of the church asked me to speak on Sunday morning and on the following four nights of revival services. Whenever I traveled to these types of events, my primary goal was to preach the Gospel each night and my secondary goal was to minister to the pastor of the church and his family. As the pastor and I were having dinner one night, he said that he wanted the two of us to go visit a man who was an atheist. I said, "Sure, let's do it." He then told me that he does this every time an evangelist visits his church. He said, "I just tell the man that an evangelist will be speaking at our Revival services and the man has always responds with a skeptical, yet hospitable answer. "Bring the evangelist to see me; I can handle him!"

The day came to visit him, and both the pastor and I walked up to his front door. The screen door was slightly ajar. We tapped on it and heard a voice yell from the back to come in.

When we walked in, we found him lying on the sofa, looking very pale and weak. Reluctantly, I introduced myself. I had a million thoughts running through my mind, convinced that my visit was not going to be profitable. However, I noticed there was an open Bible on the coffee table. Everything the pastor had told me indicated that this man was not interested in the gospel. So why was he reading a Bible?

Before I could say anything else, he said, "I knew you guys were coming, and I do have a question for you. I just got back from the hospital. I've got cancer. I'm getting treatment, which is why I feel so weak and puny today. I'm beginning to see how mortal and vulnerable I really am. Over the last month or so, I've been having all of these doubts and questions,

*You do not know the full scope of God's plan; your job is merely to be obedient to Him and talk to the people He is going to put in your life.*

wondering what will happen after I die. So I went to the bookstore and bought this Bible. I've been looking for the answers that you've told me were in here. But I can't find any of the answers. Can you tell me what your God says about my situation and what I should do?"

The pastor, who had tried to evangelize this man year after year, was stunned and speechless! I jumped right in and said, "I would be glad to show you what God says in your Bible." I opened up his Bible and began to show him passages about connecting with Jesus Christ. He was all ears! He immediately prayed to receive Christ when I invited him to do so.

God had prepared this man for our visit. The pastor and I didn't know what would happen—we expected a skeptical and mocking response—but God had been working on him, preparing him for that very moment. You do not know the full scope of God's plan; your job is merely to be obedient to Him and talk to the people He is going to put in your life.

There have been many times when I've talked with someone who was not initially open to the gospel message. I try always to say to them, "That's okay. I'm still going to be your friend because I love you. Whether you choose to believe this or not, I love you." Oftentimes, the next time I see that person, he is open to discussing the matter further. It's an amazing change. He will often have lots of questions to ask me about God and the Bible, questions that often take me by surprise. It's amazing what happens when I remain committed to maintaining a relationship while waiting on God to set up the Divine appointment.

The speed bump of resistance to the Gospel is an opportunity for God to work on me. He is changing me by getting me outside of my comfort zone. At the same time, God is setting up divine appointments with people who want to know how to connect with Jesus Christ. God is constantly working!

If you regularly attend church, I'll bet that you have your usual seat that you sit in week after week. Have you ever thought to ask God about what seat to sit in. Has it occurred to you that there may be someone He has been preparing all week and intended for you to speak to at the service? Are you more concerned about getting a great seat or sitting next to the one God has planned your Divine appointment with?

On one occasion, a guest at church said to me, "I really love your church. I really enjoyed the music and message. But when I sat down, someone said to me, 'Hello, I'm glad you're here, but you're sitting in my seat.'" Ouch! That's definitely no way to treat a guest. Perhaps this was God's way to get the "owner of the seat" to move to another seat so he wouldn't miss his divine appointment.

You see how easy it is to miss God's Divine appointment? You don't know who it is that God wants to put in your life today. You come to church on Sundays, wanting to worship, hear from God, study the Word, and sing praises to Him. That's great! But you need to ask one more question. You need to ask God whom it is that He wants you to sit next to or talk to. You may have no idea who that person is; you have no idea what a smile, a handshake, or a friendly "Hello! I'm so glad to see you!" could do to someone whom God has been working on. When you arrive at church each week for the worship services, you should be scoping out the place and asking God "Who do you want me to talk to? Where do you want me to sit this week?"

There will always be people who come into church with all sorts of questions and no answers. They are hoping that they will find someone who will befriend them, talk to them, and perhaps even answer some of their questions. How will you know that you are the one God wants to use unless you are on alert, praying that you don't miss the divine appointment He has scheduled?

When you walk in the doors of your church, look around, introduce yourself, and be friendly. Take a chance and ask someone if you can sit next him or her. You just might be surprised where it leads.

The lesson to learn from Ananias is to expect God to prepare others for your obedience.

## 5. Moving outside your comfort zone will always be risky.
In Acts 9:13-14 Ananias responded to God:

> *"But Ananias answered, "Lord, I have heard from many about this man, how much harm he did to Your saints at Jerusalem; ¹⁴ and here he has authority from the chief priests to bind all who call on Your name."*

Ananias was simply being honest with God! He knew Saul had authorized and observed the killing of Stephen, and he did not want to be another notch in Saul's belt. God was pushing Ananias out of his comfort zone. God's plan seemed too risky for Ananias—he even feared for his life!

*Whenever God pushes you beyond your comfort zone, you will always be able to find a reason not to do it.*

Whenever God pushes you beyond your comfort zone, you will always be able to find a reason not to do it. In fact, your rationale will always sound valid and reasonable in your own mind. God's call for obedience will not often feel good nor be convenient. But that's not the issue; it's not about your feelings or if you like God's plan. God wants you to trust Him, not your feelings. God is faithful, never changing; your feelings change all the time. So you must trust God and say to Him: "God, I'm going to do what You've called me to do and be the person You've created me to be, regardless of what I am feeling right now."

If you do this, you will begin to see amazing results. You will see many people turn their lives over to Jesus Christ and, as a result, it will ultimately impact our nation and world. But you must be willing to step outside your comfort zone.

God's plan may seem too risky for you. However, He never said following Him would be a life without risk. He has never promised His followers a life of ease, comfort, or pleasure. He certainly has not promised a life without suffering. As long as you are on this earth, there will be suffering.

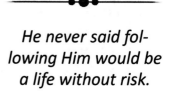

*He never said following Him would be a life without risk.*

The Scriptures do not promise an easy life once you place your faith in Jesus. In fact, it states quite the opposite. Many early Christians died because of their loyalty to Jesus Christ. It is no different today. The persecution of Christians is widespread. Christian martyrs are dying daily in our world today. It's getting worse as time proceeds. In fact, there have been more than 45 million martyrs for Christ who have died in the past 100 years. (World Christian Trends by David Barrett)

God's plans for some of you will involve pain, suffering, and great sacrifice. He knows who you are and is preparing you for those moments. He wants to be your strength at that time. When you step outside your comfort zone and obey God, you can expect that He will honor His commitment to you.

*This may surprise you, and even anger you, but our personal comfort is not God's great concern.*

You may be hesitant to step out of your comfort zone because you believe God would never want you to suffer. You may think God would never expect you to take risks. You may find it inconceivable that God would ask you to do something that might result in the loss of your reputation or treasured possessions.

You may think that God would never allow you to be humiliated before others, including non-believers.

This may surprise you, and even anger you, but our personal comfort is not God's great concern. His burden is for the great numbers of people who are lost and disconnected from Him. His purpose on earth for each of us involves His plan for reconciliation. He has already paid the debt of our sins. He has offered forgiveness and a new life to all. And, He has commissioned His followers to get that message out, regardless of the cost to you personally.

Our discomfort or suffering may be just what is needed to slow us down long enough to experience God. The pain may be what is necessary for you to grow spiritually and experience intimacy with God. God is not about to change His plan. You are His plan for calling people back to a relationship with Him. Moving outside of your comfort zone will always be risky business, but if it's God's plan, it is certainly worth pursuing. That's why God is more than willing to place such a speed bump in your path.

**6. God will give you courage to go outside your comfort zone.**
When you focus on God's ultimate objective, it produces courage for you to move beyond your comfort zone. Remember, Ananias told God how nervous he was about going to see Saul. Let's look at God's answer in the next verse:

> *"But the Lord said to him, 'Go, for he is a chosen instrument of Mine, to bear My name before the Gentiles and kings and the sons of Israel; $^{16}$ for I will show him how much he must suffer for My name's sake.'"* (Acts 9:15-16 NASB)

What gave Ananias the courage to do what was very uncomfortable for him? He knew that, ultimately, it was going to result in the accomplishment of God's plan and he trusted

God's plan. He knew that what God had in store was always best. So he obeyed God, even though it appeared that it was going to cause him some pain to do so.

We often sacrifice today because we understand the future benefits of tomorrow. Parents often deny themselves today so that their children can thrive tomorrow. They often deny themselves immediate gratification so that they can invest in their kids' future (*think college*). As a nation, Americans also make great sacrifices for the greater good. Men and women of our armed forces often lay their lives on the line to establish and maintain the freedoms of other people in other nations. Why make that sacrifice? Because we know that the world will ultimately be a better place to live as a result of the sacrifices that are made today.

> *We often sacrifice today because we understand the future benefits of tomorrow.*

Ultimately, this is what God is saying. Sacrifices and suffering are non-negotiable parts of His plan in our fallen world. God is not committed to preserving your comfort zone. A prayer dialogue with God will always reveal God's everlasting commitment to restoring and redeeming man's relationship with Himself. The consequences of sin unfortunately require this. Therefore, you must resist being shortsighted and unwilling to accept any reason to suffer or sacrifice for the accomplishment of God's bigger plan. Begin to look beyond yourself.

Think about what God is up to in your family's life. What role are you meant to fill? Think about what God wants to do in your workplace. What role are you meant to fill? Think about God's role for you in your neighborhood. How does God plan to use you to

> *Sacrifices and suffering are non-negotiable parts of His plan in our fallen world.*

be part of the redemption process there? What might God be requiring of you to affect that kind of change? You can count on God to give you the courage to move outside your comfort zone.

Maybe God is telling you to go talk to that person you work with about Jesus. Maybe you're nervous about it, and thinking, "No, no, I'm not ready for that."

Take a look at the big picture. What will happen if they never hear about Jesus? What could happen if they do hear about God's love and grace? Hopefully this encourages you to take the initiative and reach outside your comfort zone.

Do you still need some more courage? Listen to the psalmist and do what he did.

- **Are you approaching God every morning, eagerly waiting to hear from Him?**

  *"In the morning, O LORD, You will hear my voice; in the morning I will order my prayer to You and eagerly watch." (Psalm 5:3 NASB)*

- **God's Word doesn't say that you won't get your feet tangled and caught in the net. Rather, it says that as long as you have your eyes on Him, God will pull your feet out of the net when you do get stuck.**

  *"My eyes are continually toward the Lord, for He will pluck my feet out of the net." (Psalm 25:15 NASB)*

- **Even though there may be sacrifices, suffering, and risks in accomplishing God's plan, He will always remain your refuge and protector.**

131

*"For my eyes are toward You, O God, the Lord. In You I take refuge; do not leave me defenseless."* (Psalm 141:8 NASB)

- **If you don't have any idea of where you are going, you will wander aimlessly. You will react to whatever tantalizes you. However, if your vision is united with God's visions and plans, then you will find that you are much more focused, bold, and courageous.**

*"Where there is no vision, the people are unrestrained, but happy is he who keeps the law."* (Proverbs 29:18, NASB)

When you see what God sees, you will be empowered to go forward. Jesus said: *"But seek first His kingdom and His righteousness, and all these things will be added to you"* (Matthew 6:33 NASB). What things will be provided for you? Everyday things that you need: clothing, food, and shelter. When you seek God and His plan, He will provide the rest for you. You may ask a lot of "what if's." However, it's an issue of trusting God. Do you trust God or not? God said if you seek Him and His righteousness above all else, He will take care of "all else." Is it risky? Sure, it is risky to move outside of your comfort zone. But it is necessary. God will provide you the courage to do so, just as He did Ananias.

## 7. Obedience to God results in changed lives.

Whenever you are willing to step outside of your comfort zone and obey God, you will see lives changed! *"And immediately there fell from his eyes something like scales, and he regained his sight, and he got up and was baptized;"* (Acts 9:18). Because Ananias was willing to touch Saul (physically and spiritually), Saul was radically changed. He was changed so much that he wanted to identify himself with the One who he once sought to defy. He was then baptized in the name of the One he had lived to oppose. What a radical change of life! That's the kind of life that God wants you to live when you step outside of your comfort zone.

A while ago a precious young lady, whose dad attends the church I pastor, died unexpectedly. This woman loved the Lord; and her father was also a faithfully committed Christian. But now she was gone, and the medical doctors had no idea what caused it. A family was left trying to make sense out of a situation that doesn't make any sense. After her death, they were discovering things about her faith that they didn't know. Her family didn't realize how passionate she was about sharing her faith with others at work. They learned that she was very outspoken about her faith in Jesus Christ. Many people came to the funeral service and told her dad that she had been responsible for leading them to Jesus Christ.

It was encouraging for the family members left behind to know that she had that kind of relationship with God. Now she is with Jesus. Her family wanted her funeral to be a celebration of life and that was exactly what happened. Many people testified about the impact she had had in their lives. She had shared with lots of people who were not immediately open or responsive, but they continued to listen to her because they knew she genuinely loved them.

At the funeral service I invited those who attended to respond to God by initiating a prayer dialogue. This prayer included an admission of a need for forgiveness, a belief in Christ's redemptive work on the cross, and a repentant cry to God to save them. Many prayed and invited Jesus Christ to come into their lives. I closed the service by asking those who had made this request and commitment to share it with a family member.

That night, about 10 p.m. the family was gathered together. They were crying, laughing, and reliving past memories. Then, suddenly, her phone beeped. A family member picked it up, and it was a text message from one of her friends. It said, "Hey, I just needed to talk to you. I know you're gone, but I wanted to be sure to let you know that what you said to me made a difference, and I did pray to receive Christ today."

Her friend didn't realize anyone else would see it, but her dad texted back. Now, a relationship has developed. Even in a tragic death, someone was able to come to Christ. There is no way that she could have ever known that was going to happen. She genuinely loved the person while still alive. She wasn't willing to remain in her comfort zone; she passionately told others about Christ!

That's the kind of life that God wants all of us to live. A life that is full of purpose and compassion for people. A life that is not just interested in being comfortable. God wants you to connect with Him. He wants your life to result in connecting others to Christ. Obedience to God is always going to require that you step outside of your comfort zone. The amazing result will always be changed lives.

### 8. Your obedience to God will empower others.

If you are obedient to God and step outside of your comfort zone, you may experience some angst, pain, and suffering. However, when you touch someone's life, it will ultimately touch someone else's life, which will ultimately touch someone else's life. You will empower others to move outside their comfort zones, resulting in connecting many others to Jesus Christ.

That's what happened to Ananias in Acts 9:19-21:

> *"and he took food and was strengthened. Now for several days he was with the disciples who were at Damascus, [20] and immediately he began to proclaim Jesus in the synagogues, saying, "He is the Son of God."* [21] *All those hearing him continued to be amazed, and were saying, "Is this not he who in Jerusalem destroyed those who*

134

*called on this name, and who had come here for
the purpose of bringing them bound before the
chief priests?"*

Because of Ananias' obedience and willingness to step outside of his comfort zone, he touched a man's life that ultimately touched many, many other people's lives, including yours and mine. Be willing to step outside of your comfort zone. The chain reaction will be multiplied over and over again. You will empower others who will empower others—for future generations!

### How will you respond?

How will the *Prayer Dialogue* of Ananias—one man who moved outside of his comfort zone to obey God and empower others—impact you today? It may be simply praying a prayer to God to receive Christ. After reading this chapter, you know Jesus died for you on a cross, rose from the grave, and is alive today offering you the gift of eternal life. It's simply a matter of receiving that gift and choosing to follow him the rest of your life. It may be difficult; it may be contrary to what you have been taught by your family; it may not be a popular choice among your friends.

But take the step that will change your life forever—eternally!

As you begin to live and follow Jesus, He will lead you to people and expect you to initiate conversations them, love them genuinely, and help them connect to Him. You also will run into people who don't want to have anything to do with God. Don't take it personally. They're not rejecting you. They're rejecting the One who is seeking to know them—Jesus. Your objective is just to be available anytime, anywhere. Who is it that God wants you to reach out to? If each of us were to take this seriously in the next few weeks, they wouldn't all fit inside our churches across America. What a problem to have!

Don't wait—start today! Jump out of your comfort zone and reach out to as many people as you can. Are you ready? There are two questions to ask yourself to determine if you are ready to step outside your comfort zone:

- *__Have you ever connected with Jesus Christ?__* Do you only know a lot of things about Him, or have you personally connected with Him, admitting you are a sinner and inviting Him to forgive your sins and change your life? No one else can do this for you; you have to do it for yourself. If you have placed your faith in Him alone, He's there ... for good. If you've not connected with Him, do it now. You will be radically changed.

  Step outside of your comfort zone of skepticism and doubt. Take a step of faith in the direction of Jesus Christ. Once you do, take more steps out of your comfort zone in order to be used by God for His plan.

- *__Who has God put in your life?__* Is there someone you need to impact, touch, love, and encourage? Who is in your life that you need to talk to about your relationship with Christ? Make a list and begin talking with them one by one.

## QUESTIONS FOR PERSONAL EVALUATION AND DISCUSSION:

1. What is the importance of cultivating a lifestyle prayer dialogue? Why and how would a prayer monologue hinder your spiritual growth?
2. Are you a disciple? What would you say are the characteristics of a disciple?
3 According to page 116 have you ever read a part of Scripture and felt like it was a personal message to you? Share with your group the scripture passage and how it was affected you.

**PRAYER:**

*Heavenly Father, thank You for the role model that Ananias is to us. I can see myself throughout his Prayer Dialogue of reluctance to go outside my comfort zone and obey You. But I also know that You've created us to make a difference in others' lives. Grant me courage to move forward and step out of my comfort zone daily to impact those around me. You want to use me Lord ... help me to be willing to be used by You.*

# ANANIAS

## SPEED BUMPS

- The reputation of Saul filled Ananias with fear and reluctance

---

## WHAT IS NECESSARY TO CHANGE YOUR PRAYER MONOLOGUE INTO A PRAYER DIALOGUE?

Be willing to move outside your comfort zone when obedience to God demands it.

## Chapter 7

# NEGOTIATING WITH GOD: GIDEON

A s a child, I used to watch the television game show hosted by Monte Hall called "Let's Make a Deal." Each contestant began by trading a personal item for some money, an unopened package or sealed envelope. Then Monte offered another deal before you could open that envelope or package. His second offer was disguised as something better or worse than the first. You had to guess which deal was the best deal. The problem was you still didn't know what you were getting until after you made the deal. Then you were stuck with whatever you traded for. The fatter envelope that appeared to have more money in it often had less. The curtain that covered a room big enough to contain a new car was often opened to reveal a small kitchen appliance or dog biscuit.

People are always trying to get a better deal. While trading for something that appears better, you often settle for something much worse. To avoid a path that looks much too difficult to travel, you will often end up on another path that leads to nowhere. Unfortunately, this is quite common in the way you and I treat God.

### *The Speed Bump: Negotiating With God*

We are often guilty of treating God like He is some sort of game show host. When He speaks to you and gives instruction about how to live, you respond like His offer can be traded in for what's behind curtain 1 or curtain 2. It's true; you do have choices in life but those choices involve dialogues with God that are really issues of obedience or disobedience; trust and distrust. Your insistence on negotiating a better deal may actually result in the construction of a speed bump that slows or redirects your spiritual growth journey and intimacy with God. That's what happened in the life of the last biblical character we will now study. His name was Gideon.

### *God Is Speaking In The Speed Bump*

Gideon was an expert negotiator; or at least so he tried to be. He had an ongoing dialogue with God that revealed an inner restlessness with many questions. When God eventually instructed Him, he continually sought to negotiate another deal. You are about to see how his attempts to negotiate with God revealed His lack of faith in God. Let's look at the *Prayer Dialogue* Gideon had with God and learn how to maneuver past the speed bump of negotiation to arrive at true intimacy with God.

### *How To Make The Most Of This Speed Bump*

### 1. Let the pressure you are feeling create a desire for change in your relationship with God.

Gideon lived during a time when God was disciplining His people for their wickedness. For seven years the Israelites suffered under the oppressive hand of the Midianites. It was God's desire that they change their ways and return to Him. Notice what it took to get the people of God to finally wake up and call out to God for help.

> *"Then the sons of Israel did what was evil in the sight of the LORD; and the LORD gave them into the hands of Midian seven years.² The power of Midian prevailed against Israel. Because of Midian the sons of Israel made for themselves the dens, which were in the mountains and the caves*

*and the strongholds. ³ For it was when Israel had sown, that the Midianites would come up with the Amalekites and the sons of the east and go against them. ⁴ So they would camp against them and destroy the produce of the earth as far as Gaza, and leave no sustenance in Israel as well as no sheep, ox, or donkey.*

*⁵ For they would come up with their livestock and their tents, they would come in like locusts for number, both they and their camels were innumerable; and they came into the land to devastate it. ⁶ So Israel was brought very low because of Midian, and the sons of Israel cried to the LORD."* Judges 6:1-6 (NASB)

The Israelites were finally ready to change. Life was very difficult. They had lost just about everything. Scripture says, *"Israel became poverty stricken."* They cried out to God that they've had enough! And how did God respond? He sent a prophet (Judges 6:7-9).

The prophet reminded the Israelites that it was God who had set them free from slavery in Egypt and gave them the land that they now possessed. In other words, God reminded them that His past record proved that He could be trusted. The prophet continued:

*"and I said to you, 'I am the LORD your God; you shall not fear the gods of the Amorites in whose land you live. But you have not obeyed Me.'"* (Judges 6:10 NASB).

This was God's way of saying, "The reason you are in this mess is because you didn't trust Me. I've done everything in My power to help you trust Me. I performed miracles; I freed your people from slavery; I gave you a whole new land to call your own. Yet you still choose to disobey Me. That is why you are suffering."

Until there is a desire for change and a restlessness concerning the "status quo," you will not be able to fully trust and obey God. As long as things are going fairly well you will continue down the same road and look for the paths of least resistance. Since God wants you to change, you can expect Him to apply pressure in your life that will first produce a desire for change. This is what happened with the Israelites. They were now ready for change; and it would ultimately impact their relationship with God.

Are you ready for a change? The duration of your situation will be dependent upon the intensity of your desire for change. Once you desire change it becomes important that you see how God has used the pressure to prepare you for a change. He wants you to learn a few indispensible truths before you move past this speed bump.

## 2. <u>Take into account how God has been preparing you for this change.</u>

God is not expecting you to change on your own. God has been and will be constantly working in your life to prepare you so you are able to trust Him. Unfortunately, that often requires painful confrontation. And God doesn't accept excuses. He wants you to come to the point where you trust Him, even when you cannot make sense of what He is doing. Let me show you how this worked in Gideon's case.

> *"Then the angel of the LORD came and sat under the oak that was in Ophrah, which belonged to Joash the Abiezrite as his son Gideon was beating out wheat in the wine press in order to save it from the Midianites. [12] The angel of the LORD appeared to him and said to him, "The LORD is*

142

*with you, O valiant warrior." <sup>13</sup> Then Gideon said to him, "O my lord, if the LORD is with us, why then has all this happened to us? And where are all His miracles, which our fathers told us about, saying, 'Did not the LORD bring us up from Egypt?' But now the LORD has abandoned us and given us into the hand of Midian.'"* Judges 6:11-13 (NASB)

This conversation between Gideon and the angel of the Lord highlights this preparation for change. By initiating the conversation with Gideon, the angel provoked a few emotional and thoughtful responses from Gideon. Before he would ever change into a man who could trust God, Gideon needed some answers. So God anticipated his questions and objections and responded in the following ways:

- **God first initiated a relationship.** Life can be very hard and cause you to become so concerned about finding ways to provide relief that you never take time to consider your relationship with God. On the other hand, when everything seems to be going well you tend to be going well you tend to think you don't need God and thus ignore Him. But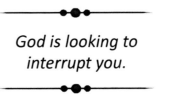

  *God is looking to interrupt you.*

  you were created by God and for God. That is why you can expect God to initiate a relationship, rather than first provide answers to your questions.

  You'll notice that God initiated a relationship with Gideon by sending an angel. This visit was unexpected. He was more concerned about hiding from the Midianites. In fact, Gideon appeared to be defensive and upset when confronted by the angel. But God was not about to let him miss this opportunity for change.

143

God is looking to interrupt you, too. You may be struggling just to keep your head above water. You may be experiencing the best days of your life. In either case, if God is not a priority in your life, you can expect an interruption. God is reaching out to you. As a matter of fact, the greatest historic demonstration of this was about 2000 years ago when Jesus sacrificed His life on a cross for you—yes, for YOU. Because Jesus bore the wrath of God that all of our sins deserved, we are free to approach God by faith. Once that relationship is established by your response of faith to Him, He will teach you the next vital truth concerning His presence in your life.

- **God promises to be with you.** God does not simply make cameo appearances. His intent and promise is to be with you ... always. In Gideon's case, verse 12 states it this way: *"The Lord is with you, O valiant warrior."* The angel assured Gideon that God was with him. Gideon's issue of trust with God was not to be based on a vague memory

  *God does not simply make cameo appearances.*

  of a one-time encounter but rather of an ongoing and current relationship with God. An angel assured Gideon that God would be with him wherever God might lead him. This same assurance is given to you. God's presence in your life is guaranteed the moment you place your faith in Jesus Christ.

- **God will give you a glimpse of His plan for your life.** God created you and has a purpose for your life. This purpose, when known, will require that you trust God. Notice again what the angel said to Gideon in verse 12:

*"The Lord is with you, O valiant warrior."* Gideon was not an experienced warrior. He was a farmer doing whatever he could to simply survive. Yet, God declared him to be a "valiant warrior." God was giving Gideon a brief look into the future.

That is the way God will work with you, as well. He will give you a glimpse of what He wants to do in your life. That brief glimpse often appears impossible to you because it is nothing like you expected. God is committed to preparing you for His plan for your life.

*God is committed to preparing you for His plan for your life.*

He is not going to ask you to do something that He has not already prepared you for. You will simply need to trust Him.

- ***God will not answer all of your questions ahead of time***. Gideon tried to get all of his questions answered by the angel. The conversation went something like this: "Please, sir. If the Lord is willing to be with us, why has all this happened? Why don't we see powerful signs like our fathers saw and told us about? Why has the Lord abandoned us and handed us over to Midian!" Gideon was full of questions for God. But God did not feel inclined to answer them at this time. God will not give you all the answers to your questions either, before you are required to trust Him. God wants you to take a step of faith; He's not going to let you in on everything before His plan unfolds.

- ***God will always provide what you need to take the next step***. God knew Gideon felt inadequate for the task. He knew Gideon didn't feel like a mighty warrior. But God

145

made sure that Gideon knew what the next step would be. God gave Gideon all he could handle; nothing more, nothing less.

So what was Gideon's next step to be? Verse 14 tells us that God told him to *"deliver Israel."* Plain and simple! God wanted Gideon to deliver Israel. I'm sure Gideon was wondering if he had just clearly heard God. *Really, God? Deliver the entire nation of Israel? ME?* That's why God immediately reminded him that He was the sender. It was to be an issue of trust; not competence or personal ability. Verse 14 says, *"Deliver Israel from the hand of Midian. Have I not sent you?"*

Perhaps you currently face a decision and are wondering, *"What am I going to do?"* God has provided you enough grace to take the very next step. Not the next five steps … just the next *one*. Verse 14 says, *"The Lord looked at him and said, 'Go in this your strength.' "* What does that mean? You are to do the best you can but also realize your best will not be enough. His presence and His command will be enough.

God understands that you will have doubts about whether or not you can accomplish His plan. However, remember that He will be with you and will empower you to carry out His plan for you. God is looking for somebody who will trust Him, obey Him, and be willing to take that first step of faith without first requiring the answers to all his questions.

### 3. Anticipate feelings of inadequacy.

Read how Gideon felt inadequate in verse 15: *"He said to Him, 'O Lord. How shall I deliver Israel? Behold, my family is the least in Manasseh, and I am the youngest in my father's house."* Gideon asks, *Why me? I can't do this!* Have you ever felt that way? It is very possible—no, probable—that you will feel inadequate to accomplish the plan God has set forth. In fact, you might as well expect it! Because what God is planning to do is much bigger than you. You should always feel inadequate in comparison to God's master plan.

These feelings and emotions are a vital part of the preparation before He does something spectacular in your life. It is a process you must go through. So when that moment happens, listen to God and follow His lead.

## 4. Remember God's bottom-line: His Presence is Enough.

God's plan is not about your abilities. It also doesn't have anything to do with your attitude and thoughts about whether or not you think you can do it. It has everything to do with Him, His presence, and His power. Verse 16, *"Surely I will be with you, and you shall defeat Midian as one man."* God told Gideon that when He does something, it doesn't matter whether there is one person involved or thousands. People tend to evaluate the success of a plan based upon their own abilities. Here we see God telling Gideon that His ability to defeat the Midianites would be as simple as Gideon's to defeat one person. Gideon could handle one person.

By the way, you can handle your "one person," too! There is no problem too big that God cannot handle in your life. When He is involved, it's a done deal, if you're willing to trust Him. Nothing else matters except God's presence in your life.

## 5. Know that God understands your need for assurance.

You, most likely, will argue with God. You will likely say something similar to this: "God, I am having a hard time believing this. I know what You are asking me to do, and that You are telling me to trust You. You're saying that You are going to be present and that Your presence will be enough. I see all that, but can't we do it some other way? Or can't You just do this without me?"

Read verses 17-21:

*"So Gideon said to Him, "If now I have found favor in Your sight, then show me a sign that it is You who speak with me. ¹⁸ "Please do not depart from here, until I come back to You, and bring out my offering and lay it before You." And He said, "I will remain until you return." ¹⁹ Then Gideon went in and prepared a young goat and unleavened bread from an ephah of flour; he put the meat in a basket and the broth in a pot, and brought them out to him under the oak and presented them. ²⁰ The angel of God said to him, "Take the meat and the unleavened bread and lay them on this rock, and pour out the broth." And he did so. ²¹ Then the angel of the LORD put out the end of the staff that was in his hand and touched the meat and the unleavened bread; and fire sprang up from the rock and consumed the meat and the unleavened bread. Then the angel of the LORD vanished from his sight."*

So Gideon began negotiating with God: *"If You do this, and if You do that, then I will know You are God."* What happened? Gideon got what he asked for! Suddenly, the fire consumed his sacrifice. He was shocked! Next the angel was gone ... vanished from his sight.

Verse 22 continues,

*"When Gideon saw that he was the angel of the LORD, he said, "Alas, O Lord GOD! For now I have seen the angel of the LORD face to face.' "*

Why did Gideon say that? It was believed in Gideon's time that if one ever had an encounter with God and you looked at Him face-to-face as you would one of your peers, then you would die.

This revealed that Gideon didn't trust God all along—until it was almost too late. Gideon talked to this representative from God, the angel, casually like he did because he didn't realize he was an angel of the Lord. He didn't truly believe that God was going to show up and do anything. All of a sudden, it dawned on him: it had been God! Then he thought he was going to die for treating God so flippantly.

Interestingly enough, God addresses this in verse 23: *"Peace to you. Do not fear; you shall not die."* During moments of negotiating, God says, "I understand. What you did is not right. It's not appropriate. It doesn't honor Me or respect Me, but I understand. You are weak and timid and insecure. You really want to believe, but you don't. You want to trust, but you don't. But you do not

*God is always going to deal with your insecurities by revealing Himself.*

need to fear; I will not destroy you. I desire peace to be upon you." God even takes it one step further in verse 24: *"So Gideon built an altar there to the Lord there and named it The LORD is Peace."* He named it after God. God's name here in Hebrew was Yahweh Shalom. Translated this meant the God of peace, the peaceful God, the God who relented from judgment at that moment.

God is always going to deal with your insecurities by revealing Himself. God's name is Yahweh Shalom, the God of peace. He wants you to know Him as that. He wants you to know His name. Because He is the God of peace, God understood Gideon's insecurities. What about your insecurities? God understands those, too. But He still wants you to stop negotiating with Him so you can truly know Him as the God of peace.

### 6. Expect God's plan to impact your relationships with others.

Now that God had revealed to Gideon that he was Yahweh Shalom, the God of peace, it was time to get to work—God

149

had a task for him to accomplish. Gideon was to go to the top of the mountain to the altar of the false god Baal. This altar belonged to Gideon's father, Joash. God instructed Gideon to destroy the altar and offer a sacrifice to God on a new altar in its place.The Bible says that Gideon was a little nervous about God's plan because the pagan altar had belonged to his dad and he knew that everyone in the community would be upset that he destroyed it. You can imagine his anxiety. So Gideon waited until night to complete the task.

The next day the sun came up, and people realized the old altar was gone and a new one existed in its place—and they were angry! They demanded to know who did it. When they got word it was Gideon, they searched for Joash, Gideon's father, and demanded Gideon's death. Joash replied:

> "But Joash said to all who stood against him, "Will you contend for Baal, or will you deliver him? Whoever will plead for him shall be put to death by morning. If he is a god, let him contend for himself, because someone has torn down his altar." 32 Therefore on that day he named him Jerubbaal, that is to say, "Let Baal contend against him," because he had torn down his altar." (verses 31-32)

Do you see how God's will for Gideon impacted his relationship with his father, not to mention the entire community? When you trust and obey God, you are going to impact others; some positively, some negatively.

### 7. Know that God will always empower you to do His will at just the right time.

Verse 33 says, *"Then all the Midianites and the Amalekites, and the sons of the east assembled themselves; and they crossed over and camped in the Valley of Jezreel."* When Gideon tore down the Baal altar, the news traveled quickly to the Midianites and the other surrounding tribes, who were Baal worshippers. The tribes were so upset that they gathered all of their forces and came to fight to rebuild the altar to Baal. Verse 34 and 35 says,

> "So the Spirit of the LORD came upon Gideon; and he blew a trumpet, and the Abiezrites were called together to follow him. [35] He sent messengers throughout Manasseh, and they also were called together to follow him; and he sent messengers to Asher, Zebulun, and Naphtali, and they came up to meet them."

Because Gideon obeyed God in a "little thing" (tearing down an altar was a big thing to Gideon but only one little step of obedience to God), God empowered him to take the next step. Gideon grabbed the horn, blew it, and people came from everywhere; thousands of people came ready to fight against the Midianites.

When you begin to trust God a little bit, you will begin to understand and appreciate the power of God. If you want God to do the miraculous in your life, you first must obey Him in the little things. When you trust Him with the little things, then you will be able to trust Him with the big things. That is what is happened in Gideon's life, in his *Prayer Dialogue*. However, don't assume that once that "big" thing happens that you have finally "arrived." Don't do it! Because Gideon did exactly that and blew it!

## 8. Refuse to allow your doubts to keep you from trusting and obeying God.

Gideon was so full of reservations, even though God had empowered him to do the miraculous. Yet again, he tried to negotiate with God.

Verse 36 picks up the story that Gideon is most remembered for...the fleeces. Now remember, is there any question about what God wanted Gideon to do? No! No question at all, but what does Gideon say? He tries again to negotiate with God by inserting the word *"if."*

> *"Then Gideon said to God, 'If you will deliver Israel by my hand, as you said, I will put a fleece of wool here on the threshing floor. If dew is only on the fleece and all the other ground is dry, I will know that you will deliver Israel by my strength, as you said."* (verses 36-37)

Gideon still had his doubts. He wanted to hear again what God intended to do. And, he still hoped that God would change His mind. So Gideon, for the third time, tested God and again, tried to bargain with Him. As you can see from the following verses, God patiently guided Gideon over this speed bump.

> *"Then Gideon said to God, "And it was so. When he arose early the next morning and squeezed the fleece, he drained the dew from the fleece, a bowl full of water. Then Gideon said to God, "Do not let Your anger burn against me that I may speak once more; please let me make a test once more with the fleece, let it now be dry only on the fleece, and let there be dew on all the ground." God did so that night; for it was dry only on the fleece, and dew was on all the ground."* (verses 38-40)

Gideon was a man of God; he had a relationship with God. Like most believers, Gideon was growing in his relationship with God, but he still had doubts of all kinds. And even though God had revealed Himself to Gideon in great ways, he still had a hard time trusting God. Because of his doubts and mistrust, Gideon constantly negotiated with God. However, the great thing about God is that He is so patient! He was patient with Gideon throughout each test and negotiation in which displayed Gideon's lack of faith, trust, and obedience. God is also patient with you as you grow in your faith, trust, and obedience.

## Another Word About Fleeces

"Fleeces" are like tossing a coin the second time because you didn't like the results of the first toss. It's saying, "I don't like what God is telling me to do, so let's negotiate one more time." After God gives you guidance, the purpose of a fleece is not for clarity. Instead it reveals your desire for God to change His mind. If you don't like what God is saying, a fleece will not help.

> *"Fleeces" are like tossing a coin the second time because you didn't like the results of the first toss.*

Fleeces reveal a lack of maturity and a reluctance to obey God. Don't allow Gideon's use of a fleece to be a guiding principle for your life. God will put up with some of the things that all of us do in our immaturity. God didn't scold Gideon for doing it. He responded; He proved faithful. But Gideon learned from it. It is doubtful that he laid out more fleeces. Hopefully, as he grew closer and closer to God, He began to listen to God more and trust Him.

## 9. You will clear the speed bump of negotiation when your response to God is worship.

You'll know you have come to trust God when the result of your spiritual dialogue leads to worship. Gideon learned this in Judges 7. He had gathered an army of 32,000 to fight the Midianites. However, once again, God had different plans. God informed Gideon that he had too many soldiers. If the Israelites defeated the Midianites with their powerful army of 32,000, they would then boast that it was done in their own strength, not in the Lord's. Gideon would be tempted not to trust God and His plan. So God told Gideon to let any soldiers go that were fearful of fighting. How many soldiers left? Twenty-two thousand! Only 10,000 remained with Gideon.

Still, that was too many men. God told Gideon to filter out more men until only 300 remained. Imagine how Gideon, whom you now know struggled with doubts, was feeling. After having 32,000 men prepared to fight, he now had 300 men to win a battle. Needless to say, Gideon was apprehensive at best. He might have even contemplated throwing out another fleece. However, God prevailed.

> *"Now the same night it came about that the LORD said to him, 'Arise, go down against the camp, for I have given it into your hands. 10 "But if you are afraid to go down, go with Purah your servant down to the camp, 11 and you will hear what they say; and afterward your hands will be strengthened that you may go down against the camp." So he went with Purah his servant down to the outposts of the army that was in the camp.'"* (Judges 7:9-11 NASB)

Gideon obeyed God and crept down to the enemy camp. He overheard two soldiers talking. One soldier admitted that he had a dream that the Israelites were going to destroy them! The other soldier responded,

> *"His friend replied, "This is nothing less than the sword of Gideon the son of Joash, a man of Israel; God has given Midian and all the camp into his hand."* (Judges 7:14 NASB)

154

In that moment, Gideon fully realized that God was not only working on him, but also working in the Midianite camp. Judges 7:15 says,

> *"When Gideon heard the account of the dream and its interpretation, he bowed in worship. He returned to the camp of Israel and said, "Arise, for the LORD has given the camp of Midian into your hands.'"*

Gideon *worshipped*. He immediately bowed down and worshipped God. He finally realized that God is God—greater than Gideon, greater than Gideon's plans, greater than the entire Israelite nation and greater than any obstacle that might be in the way. God's plans and His power always prevail. Worship was the final step.

The negotiating stopped when Gideon finally saw God at work. He had grown intimately aware of God's faithfulness. So he bowed reverentially and worshipped God. The speed bump was effected.

Following this important milestone, Gideon and the Israelites did, indeed, conquer the Midianites:

> *"So Midian was subdued before the sons of Israel, and they did not lift up their heads anymore. And the land was undisturbed for forty years in the days of Gideon."* (Judges 8:28 NASB)

However, the more important lesson was discovered within Gideon's *Prayer Dialogue with God*, whom he learned to finally trust and express that trust with obedience and worship.

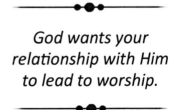

*God wants your relationship with Him to lead to worship.*

### *How will you respond?*

What is the point of Gideon's *Prayer Dialogue*? God wants your relationship with Him to lead to worship. Do you want to know how to trust God? Do you want to know how to stop negotiating and start trusting Him? You will know that you are making progress and growing exponentially when your obedience to God leads to worship. Worship is not just something that you do on a Sunday morning in a sanctuary filled with people and music and preaching. Worship happens whenever the Holy Spirit impresses Himself on you and you feel compelled to respond. Worship is showing your love for God; it is declaring God's worth and holiness. Whenever God reveals Himself to you as a God who has everything in control and you respond to Him with praise and thanksgiving, you have worshipped Him.

Worship should naturally lead to service. Your time of worship should translate into actions—to go and do what God has commissioned you to do. That is how you grow from being a negotiator to being one who trusts and worships the one and only true God. There will always be challenges in life.

> *Your time of worship should translate into actions—to go and do what God has commissioned.*

They are intended to get your attention. They are speed bumps intended to slow you down long enough to pay attention to God. May Gideon's example encourage you as you seek to move beyond negotiating with God about a change of plans to knowing and worshipping the one true God.

## QUESTIONS FOR PERSONAL EVALUATION AND DISCUSSION:

1. "Until there is a desire for change and a restlessness concerning the "status quo," you will not be able to fully

trust and obey God." (Page 137) What change in your life needs to take place for you to fully trust and obey God?

2. God does not promise us the full knowledge and blueprint of His plans. Are you willing to live a life abandoned to His plan, even without knowing all the answers? What do you like/dislike about this?

3. How could your trust and obedience to the Lord negatively impact others? (Page 145-146)

## PRAYER:

*Oh Father, please stop me from negotiating. I want more than the status quo. Please, wake me up so that I don't continue to treat You like You are just another man with some good ideas. Help me to treat You like You are God. Help me to trust You. Help me to worship You, so I can accomplish what You have planned—Your perfect purpose for my life. When I am at a crossroad in my life, help me resist negotiating with You and attempting to change Your mind. Help me to be bold and take the next step. Thank You for preparing me to take the next step. Thank You for Your patience. Thank You for always continuing to pour out Your grace and mercy. Finally, help me to be guided by the Holy Spirit to worship You—anytime, anywhere. I praise You, Lord!*

# GIDEON

## SPEED BUMPS

- Pay attention to God's purpose ("you are a warrior")
- Obey God in the little things
- God reduces number of soldiers necessary to 300 from 32,000

---

## WHAT IS NECESSARY TO CHANGE YOUR PRAYER MONOLOGUE INTO A PRAYER DIALOGUE?

Stop trying to negotiate with God, learn to trust Him and worship Him.

## Chapter 8

# SLOW DOWN FOR THE SPEED BUMPS

The psalmist says, "Cease striving and know that I am God; I will be exalted among the nations, I will be exalted in the earth." Psalm 46:10 (NASB) It is in your human nature to resist and fight back when someone gets in your way—even God. As you can see from the biographical studies in this book, we all tend to push back when God deals with us. You are a creature of habit and repeatedly insist on doing things your way. You speed on swerving around the potholes of life and think you're doing just fine as long as you don't get a flat tire and can keep on moving. Your interaction with God becomes nothing but a prayer monologue full of requests and demands for help in maneuvering around the potholes and navigating over the speed bumps.

Yet, God has other plans. Spiritual growth and maturity that leads to intimacy with God requires that you slow down for the strategically placed speed bumps in your life. God may even require that you come to a complete stop before you can learn the valuable truth

> *Spiritual growth and maturity that leads to intimacy with God requires that you slow down for the strategically placed speed bumps in your life.*

concerning your relationship with Him. You cannot know God the way He wants you to know Him until you "cease striving" with Him. In fact, you are encouraged by God to "consider it all joy" (James 1:2-3 NASB) when you have to slow down for the trials and tribulations you face. The joy comes in remembering the desired outcome of the speed bump. Slowing down and learning from these speed bumps will force you to carry on a prayer dialogue instead of continuing with your prayer monologue.

Let's quickly review how this worked in the lives of the biblical characters we previously looked at.

- Abraham and Sarah eventually learned to take God seriously. This occurred after Abraham's conversation with God about Sodom's fate and after the birth of his promised son, Isaac.
- Joshua went solo with God and led the Israelites into the Promised Land only after Moses was taken from him in death and after God dealt with his fears.
- Jacob finally stopped trying to manipulate people and ignore God only after spending 21 years as a bondservant to Laban and after wrestling with God resulted in a dislocated hip.
- Nehemiah was instrumental in the rebuilding of a nation after his heart was broken over his countrymen's condition and once he left his comfortable position as cupbearer of the king.
- Ananias was used to empower Paul to change the world only after choosing to obey God rather than listen to his fears.
- Gideon was able to truly worship God once he ceased trying to negotiate with God and finally obey and trust Him.

Speed bumps are an unavoidable part of life. How you maneuver over them or around them will ultimately determine the depth of your intimacy with God. Even as I write this final chapter, I'm thinking of a good friend that just found out his son attempted to take his own life. This horrible incident has definitely forced my friend and his wife to slam on the brakes and slow down for the speed bump. They have become immediately aware, because of the speed bump, of how helpless they are. It has forced upon them the need of a prayer dialogue.

If nothing else, I'm hopeful that you'll no longer see the unexpected and aggravating interruptions in your life as events to be avoided or ignored. I believe God loves us so much that He is willing to do or allow things to happen in our lives that are intended to get our attention and enable us to know and love Him. These are often painful and annoying but so necessary.

> *Speed bumps are an unavoidable part of life. How you maneuver over them or around them will ultimately determine the depth of your intimacy with God.*

Do pay attention and slow down for speed bumps. You can trust Him...so do it! He loves you... so love Him back! He began a good work in you...so let Him do it! Intimacy with God is a reality that you can experience. But you're going to have to slow down at the speed bumps.

> *"Consider it all joy, my brethren, when you encounter various trials, ³ knowing that the testing of your faith produces endurance. ⁴ And let endurance have its perfect result, so that you may be perfect and complete, lacking in nothing."*
> James 1:2-4 (NASB)

## QUESTIONS FOR PERSONAL EVALUATION AND DISCUSSION:

1. Which biographical example(s) spoke most clearly to your life, and why?
2. Since "speed bumps" are unavoidable; how can you prepare for them before they even happen?
3. What is the "speed bump" in your life right now?

**PRAYER:**

*Heavenly Father, thank you for teaching me how to slow down and appreciate the many little things that I am prone to interpret as inconvenient obstacles in my life. I tend to be in a rush all the time. Now I see the value of slowing down for the speed bumps that you place in my way. Help me to slow down at the future speed bumps that are intended to help me grow closer to you. I want to know you intimately.*

CPSIA information can be obtained at www.ICGtesting.com
Printed in the USA
LVOW06s0459300114

371534LV00006B/9/P